The Art and Strategy of Service-Learning Presentations

Second Edition

Rick Isaacson
San Francisco State University

Jeff Saperstein
San Francisco State University

THOMSON

WADSWORTH

Australia • Canada • Mexico • Singapore • Spain • United Kingdom • United States

For more information about our products, contact us at:
Thomson Learning Academic Resource Center
1-800-423-0563

For permission to use material from this text or product, submit a request online at
http://www.thomsonrights.com.
Any additional questions about permissions can be submitted by email to
thomsonrights@thomson.com.

Thomson Wadsworth
10 Davis Drive
Belmont, CA 94002-3098
USA

Asia
Thomson Learning
5 Shenton Way #01-01
UIC Building
Singapore 068808

Australia/New Zealand
Thomson Learning
102 Dodds Street
Southbank, Victoria 3006
Australia

Canada
Nelson
1120 Birchmount Road
Toronto, Ontario M1K 5G4
Canada

Europe/Middle East/South Africa
Thomson Learning
High Holborn House
50/51 Bedford Row
London WC1R 4LR
United Kingdom

Latin America
Thomson Learning
Seneca, 53
Colonia Polanco
11560 Mexico D.F.
Mexico

Spain/Portugal
Paraninfo
Calle/Magallanes, 25
28015 Madrid, Spain

Acknowledgements

The authors would like to acknowledge the following contributors to this text:

Jeanne Jacobs for her contribution to the section on "Alternative Message Forums for Community Activism" in Chapter 5; Dr. Bruce Dorries and Dr. Kevin Brown for their contributions to this text from the first edition; Dr. Tom Peters, Executive Director of the Marin Community Foundation, for providing access to his speeches and reflections on leadership; Mya Kramer, President of M Line, for her insights on the creative process and permission to use products she produced for Glide Memorial Church; Jennifer Nelson and Amanda McCall for their assistance in obtaining graphics from the "We Want Change" campaign; Linda Compton, Executive Director of Whistlestop in Marin for her help; and Scott Henry from the Marin Independent Journal for his assistance in obtaining our cover photo.

CONTENTS

PREFACE

Let no one ever come to you without leaving better and happier
Mother Teresa (1910-1997)

Service-learning challenges students to perform meaningful service in their communities while engaging in academic reflection and study related to their activities. Beyond applying classroom skills in an applied setting, our goal is to cultivate your sense of community involvement and higher social purpose, giving even greater value to the communication skills you acquire. Service-learning reflects the philosophy that learning, to be most effective, should be linked to social and civic responsibility. The best learning is active and connected to meaningful experience with others.

Our first edition, *Service-Learning in Communication Studies,* examined the broad integration of the speech communication discipline with service-learning. While again providing a history, guidelines and resources for service-learning, this second edition focuses more specifically on presentational speaking and varied forms of public communication. Our view is that traditional platform speaking is limited to one method of public communication. In addition to supplementing concepts and theories that you are presently using to develop informative and persuasive presentations, this text extends the traditional domain of public speaking to reflect the versatile nature of contemporary communication. Accordingly, we devote chapters to alternative message forums and methods, including guerrilla media, public service announcements, techniques of effective advertising, and oral interpretation. Given the symbolic and organizational need to spearhead service programs, we also present a chapter on speaking as a community leader. This unit covers the rhetoric of both national and local leaders. We assess their rhetorical strategies and provide exercises that will help you hone your ability to speak as a leader.

Addressing a critically important but often neglected skill, we also devote a chapter to transactional communication, recognizing that public communication transcends the one-way channel of speaker addressing audience. Interactively communicating with agency staff, peers, and those served in the field, demands an ability to incorporate listening and spontaneously adapting to a variety of fluid communication situations.

The second edition also emphasizes the importance of creating visually rich messages by incorporating descriptive language and integrating iconic images, advertising theory, and compelling graphics. Visualization helps audiences place a human face on social problems and creates a more vivid sense of setting and community need.

To reinforce your command of this varied range of skills, learning activities are liberally provided throughout the performance-based chapters. These exercises realistically place you in a variety of service scenarios, ranging from literacy and homeless programs to ecological, arts, and political action campaigns. The illustrative examples and exercises will enhance your understanding of the range and function of service agencies that operate in your community.

Service-learning public communication projects require you to play an active part in your community. You will probably research a topic of relevance to a nonprofit agency, organize and adapt information on the topic for a specific audience outside the classroom, and then develop and deliver a presentation or campaign that will directly benefit your community. Projects can call for speeches, group presentations, symposiums (multiple individuals presenting speeches on a common topic), and electronically mediated messages. Such presentations will give you an excellent opportunity to polish and expand your communication skills in a professional setting, even laying groundwork for your career development. There is strong empirical evidence that the communication skills and experiences one obtains from service work is valued by employers and better prepares you for a productive career in the workplace, whether you choose the nonprofit, public or private sectors.

The concluding chapter provides websites of prominent service agencies and resource guides to help you gain additional perspective of the national service-learning movement.

This text strives to meld speech communication skills with an appreciation of volunteer service, and to create a deeper understanding of the dynamics of the nonprofit sector and its broad role in influencing public policy, and its immediate task of serving individuals. Our hope is that you will expand your public communication skills, become active in volunteer service, understand your role and ability to influence public policy, and serve those in need.

CHAPTER 1

SERVICE-LEARNING IN PERSPECTIVE

This book offers you, the student, an introduction to the idea and practice of service-learning. It is our hope that after reading this book you will understand the idea of service-learning, know how to go about it, and be enthusiastic about your potential service-learning. This may be your first introduction to the term service-learning, or you may have participated in a previous service-learning experience. Either way, we hope to offer you a chance to better understand the practice of service and offer you some practical suggestions on how to go about it. The first question we will address is the most basic: what is service-learning?

THE DEFINITION AND GOALS OF SERVICE-LEARNING

Service-learning is a term that has evolved to describe a set of practices that involve students in various interactions with the community. Service-learning as an educational concept has roots in many educational traditions. Since the early 20th century educators have called for education that involved students in their communities. Educators in various ways throughout the century answered the call for education that involved students in the community. Some of the movements that arose in response include civics education, experiential education, internships, co-ops, and life-experience credits. While you may, or may not, have heard of these movements, the movement we now call service-learning started in the 1980s. The movement started in response to the general impression that college students were disengaged from their communities, self-centered, and unprepared to participate in the civic or social life of their communities (Ehrlich, 1999; Hepburn, 1997).

1

Whether justified or not, these impressions caused college administrators and others concerned about the decline in civic participation to establish the service-learning movement. Others who joined the movement included those whose primary concern was the quality of education and educational reform and advocates for social causes and volunteerism. This coalition advanced service-learning as a solution to the disconnection between the experiences of college students and the world around them.

College students were also often seen as academically prepared but with little real knowledge or concern about their obligations as citizens. For many, this also translated to the general feeling that students were unprepared for the "real world." They felt that students, though often academically excellent, made little connection between the theoretical concepts learned in the classroom and the application of those concepts (Campus Compact, 1999). The theme of student apathy converged in the late 1980s with a concern for practical learning and experience, resulting in what we currently call service-learning. It is important for you to understand the background of service-learning since there are many types of experiential education that are similar. Because of this, we will spend some time defining service-learning.

Defining Service-learning

Because of the diversity of service-learning practices it is difficult to provide a simple definition of service-learning. Service-learning is practiced and defined in many different ways by many different people. In a recent article, researchers (Shumer & Belbas, 1996) identified 26 separate forms of service-learning. This leads to a bewildering array of individual interpretations of what constitutes service-learning. However, definitions of service-learning do share some common qualities.

The most obvious thing that the various definitions of service-learning share is the need to define a term that is made up of two words, service and learning. While this may seem simplistic, the difference in the various definitions results from how the terms are treated and the varying emphasis on one term or the other. Some definitions concentrate on service, others concentrate on learning. Most, however, focus on what the learner gains through the experience. Here is an example of that type.

Example 1.1

> *Service-learning is the various pedagogies that link community service and academic study so that each strengthens the other.... The interaction with knowledge and skills is key to learning....Learning starts with a problem and continues with the*

application of increasingly complex ideas and increasingly sophisticated skills to increasingly complex problems.

This definition focuses on the benefits the learner gains from engaging in service-learning. These benefits, though they are many, are not the whole picture. Service is just as, or more important to some, as the learning. Here is an example that focuses on the service aspect of service-learning.

Example 1.2
> *"...service is the applications of one's gifts, skills, and resources to provide something of value, to enhance the quality of life of people who articulate a need or desire for service."*

In this definition you can clearly see the focus on service as the most important aspect of community service. Most definitions mention both aspects of service-learning. However, most definitions are written by academics. Academics, not surprisingly, usually focus on the learning aspect of service-learning. Despite these differences, some basics about what service-learning is about can be derived from the definitions.

What Service-learning Is
The first area of agreement between the competing definitions of service-learning is that for an activity to be called service-learning it should include an element in which students offer their services to a community-based group. What this means is that service-learning is always community service. While this is not the whole of service-learning, it is an important element. It means that students, as part of their course responsibilities are expected to perform work off-campus at the direction of community groups. This service should directly benefit the community and originate in the expressed needs of a community group. There are many forms this service can take, and they will be explained in greater detail in Chapter 4.

The second factor that the various definitions agree upon is that the service should be connected to a formal learning experience, in most cases, a class. The service should allow the students to either, apply the concepts from the class, or to gain a deeper insight into the nature of the class material. The emphasis should be on what is learned rather than on simply documenting what was done. This means that students will be given the opportunity to reflect on what they have learned from the experience. Here is an example of this type of connection from a course.

<u>Example 1.3</u>

It is particularly important that this journal <u>not</u> be merely a description of the events of the simulations. Your journal should reflect what you have learned in the course as applied to the events of your negotiation experience. The focus should be on learning rather than on the chronicling of experience. However, description can, and must, be used to describe an event which you wish to theorize and reflect upon.

The opportunity to learn reflectively is the third element of service-learning. A service-learning course should feature assignments or class-time that allow students to make sense of their experience in a reflective manner. In other words, students should have the opportunity to think about their experience and, in either words or writing, try to understand what they have learned from what they have done. When you are fully involved, service, like communication, can be totally consuming. Often, it is only after you have finished an event that you have the time to go back over the experience in your mind. This is illustrated in Example 1.3 and 1.4.

<u>Example 1.4</u>

You will be expected to write about your actions and the possible implications of those actions for your future involvement in community service. This journal is best accomplished using a two step writing process involving the immediate writing of impressions concerning the experience and the later reflective modification of those writings. This is not an exercise in style, rather in substance. Write for understanding.

In trying to make sense of your involvement you are engaging in a reflective process. In the reflection stage of service-learning this sense-making process is directed at your service experience. Often, instructors will offer questions or course material that will help you frame your reflection.

The final characteristic of service-learning is one that is not mentioned by all those who have defined service-learning. However, a significant number of definitions mention that a goal of service-learning should be to foster civic and societal involvement. It is hoped that students will gain insights into their place within, and the nature of, society. From this perspective, successful service-learning should motivate the participant to continue in service. What is hoped is that experience with service will awaken within you a sense of civic responsibility. While not all programs aim specifically at this goal, some, like Campus Compact, an organization of university presidents, aim explicitly for this objective.

As we have explained in this section you can recognize service-learning by four characteristics. These four factors are:

1. Service-learning is an activity where students offer service in the community.
2. In service-learning, service is connected to course learning objectives.
3. In service-learning, learning is based upon structured reflection.
4. Service-learning often has the capacity to motivate the student to be more engaged in the future.

These four characteristics describe what service-learning is about. The next section talks about the difference between service-learning and other forms of experiential education.

What Service Leaning Is Not

Much of the confusion over what community service is and is not occurs because service-learning is a form of experiential education. Experiential education is a term that refers to education that uses experience outside of the school setting as part of the learning strategy. While service-learning falls into the broad category of experiential education, it should not be confused with other forms. Some common forms of experiential learning are internships and cooperative education.

Service-learning is not an internship. Internships, while valuable experiences, are not service-learning. Internships do share with service-learning an orientation towards applied learning. However, internships rarely are reflectively structured. Service-learning placements feature service from which the community benefits or which motivates students to future service. Even when internships are performed in service organizations, the focus is almost entirely on performing specific skills outside of a class experience. Service-learning, in contrast, is directly connected to the content of a particular course. The term "intern" suggests that the goal of an internship is professional preparation, an apprenticeship of sorts.

A service-learning experience is also not the same as a cooperative education experience. Co-ops can be extremely useful for preparing students for a career or to investigate a particular occupation. However, they are not service-learning. Co-ops feature actual work experience that, like internships, is often unconnected to particular course content. In cooperative education there is usually a greater emphasis on adding an academic component to the work, such as a final paper or co-op report. However, co-ops clearly do not satisfy the four requirements for service-learning.

Service-learning is sometimes confused with community service. While service-learning is community service, community service is not necessarily service-learning. We know this sounds confusing, but in practice it is really pretty simple. Service-learning is considered community service since service-learning involves serving the community. However, all community service is not service-learning. Only community service activities that feature a connection to course material and formal reflection qualify as service-learning. Community service is an integral part of service-learning, but service without an explicit and formal expectation of learning is a very different thing than service-learning.

We hope at the end of this section you have a better understanding of what constitutes service-learning, what it is, and is not. We have provided a brief synopsis of the history of service-learning, what service-learning is, and what it is not. In this next section, we will discuss the benefits and possible costs of service-learning.

THE BENEFITS OF SERVICE-LEARNING

Service-learning is one of the fastest growing teaching trends in the nation. The reason for this is that service-learning seems to offer benefits for students, teachers, the university, and the community. As the service-learning movement enters the new century and its third decade, the benefits of combining service and learning are just now coming into focus. The first area where service-learning offers benefits over traditionally structured education is for students.

The Benefits of Service-learning for Students

Service-learning clearly provides benefits for students that traditional courses cannot by promoting enriched and enhanced learning (Gray et al, 2000). Students report that service-learning helps them to understand course material much better than courses not featuring this component. Confucius expressed this idea with "*I read and I forget, I see and I remember, I do and I understand.*" Service-learning allows students to do, in other words, to apply the skills or concepts from a course in practice. This learning by doing is the basis for an increased understanding of course concepts.

Enjoyment of learning is another benefit derived from service-learning. Students report that they enjoy their service experience and are often motivated to accomplish more than they do in traditional courses. This is an example of what one student reported about a service experience.

Example 1.5

> *I think that having to go every week on a set schedule has been good for me. I usually am the kind of person that procrastinates a lot. I wanted to go every week though, it is fun. It doesn't seem like school. Since this is my last journal and I'm getting ready to write the final paper I realize that I learned a lot though. Probably more than I would have any other way because it didn't seem like I was learning, it was fun.*

This example illustrates a benefit cited in student reports of their service – they like it. It is a comment on traditional education that students often state that community integrated courses are "not like learning." This would seem to indicate that students often view learning – often class – as boring and a chore.

Students also report receiving a professional development benefit from service-learning. A student in this author's public relations course commented:

Example 1.6

> *They loved the campaign we came up with. We pitched it to them and they said they are going to do everything we suggested. Am so psyched! They even gave us a budget. I really think that I can do a PR campaign for anyone now.*

Through service-learning students gain skills, experience, and confidence in their abilities and skills. Not only do they gain skills; they also gain the ability to demonstrate those skills to prospective employers. The experience of the student cited in Example 1.6 allows her to offer a future employer concrete evidence of skills and a valuable reference. She compiled a portfolio of her work that included press releases, press kits, budgets, and a brochure produced for the organization. These materials will demonstrate her competence and experience to a future employer. She also used her supervisor in the organization as a reference that could speak to her work ethic, reliability, and talent.

Students also state that their service has prepared them to live and work in an increasingly diverse world. The nature of service means that you will often work with people who are not like you in some way. Often, students remark that learning to deal with difference is one of the central things they learn in their service. An example of this can be seen in this extract from a student's service-learning journal.

<u>Example 1.7</u>

*I was so scared when I started...I think that the biggest thing
that I learned is that people are people. I also learned that people
have differences and it's important to talk about and work out those
differences... I think I am going to volunteer there now that this class
is done, I will miss everyone there too much if I don't.*

This example illustrates that learning takes place when people are put
in situations of service. It is not unusual to have the opportunity to work with
people that differ from you in significant ways. Service offers a way to
bridge those differences and learn valuable lessons about the world and
diversity.

Finally, as the examples in this chapter aptly demonstrate, service-
learning offers the possibility for personal growth. If you view your time in
college as an opportunity to learn and grow, to emerge better able to function
in your local community and job, then service-learning offers an important
opportunity for personal growth. All of us grow when we do demanding
tasks that force us to stretch to reach our goals. Service-learning offers the
chance to enter new situations and stretch our capabilities. When we speak
of capabilities we are not just referring to technical skills or course-related
ideas. Performing service gives you an opportunity to reflect on yourself as a
person and respond to life's challenges. Your ability to handle strange
situations, to deal with diverse people, and to accomplish tasks, result from a
committed service placement. These personal attributes make you better
equipped in every aspect of your life. Becoming a better person should be
one of your goals. Like students, teachers derive specific benefits from
service-learning. In this next section we will talk about some of those
benefits.

The Benefits of Service-learning for Teachers

Like you, your instructor receives tangible benefits from participating
in service-learning. The primary concern of instructors is that you learn and
understand class material. Teachers and researchers report that students who
commit to, and fulfill their service responsibilities, learn more and retain it
longer than do students who learn by traditional methods. Instructors find
this very appealing.

Teachers also enjoy having students in class who have concrete
experience with the concepts and skills addressed in class discussion. This
enables students to contribute to the discussion and help others learn. It also

promotes more in-depth class discussion due to the increased knowledge of real contexts. This makes the instructor's job easier and more satisfying.

Instructors have also discovered service-learning has the possibility of transforming student attitudes towards learning. Through service-learning assignments students often realize that they are in control of, and responsible for, their own learning. This change in attitude leads to students dedicated to learning and demanding to be taught. For many instructors this is the ultimate reward. It is clear that students and teachers get benefits from their service-learning experience. It is also clear universities and colleges derive benefits from service-learning.

The Benefits of Service-learning for Colleges/Universities
The institution also derives a clear benefit from encouraging engagement in service-learning. One of the missions of most universities and colleges is to serve their local community. Unfortunately, most institutions of higher learning have historically neglected this mission (Campus Compact, 1999; Wutzdorff & Giles, 1997). This has caused what is called the "town-gown" division. People in local communities often see schools as almost parasitic, definitely paternalistic, and often uncaring. Service-learning is one way in which universities and colleges can break down the barriers between themselves and their surrounding communities. This is attractive to administrators at your institution. Service-learning allows institutions to serve the community directly while simultaneously performing their central mission of educating students. It is clear from the last fifteen years of experience that properly conceived and executed service-learning improves the relationship between the community and the college/university. So far, we have discussed the clear benefits to students, instructors, and institutions. The final player benefiting from the service-learning equation is the community.

The Benefits of Service-learning for Communities
The community benefit may seem obvious in service-learning (Gray et al, 2000). After all, the community gains the service of the learners. While this is an obvious and tangible benefit, it is not always the main benefit to the community. A community organization integrating service-learners into its program requires the agency's effort, money, and time. The benefit the community gains from the work performed by service-learners sometimes does not equal the effort that the organization puts into training and supervising their activities. We do not imply that the efforts of service-learners are without net value. In some instances, the participation of

service-learners makes programs possible. But it is important to point out that organizations make considerable investment in student learning. If this is true, then why do service organizations continue to almost universally welcome service-learners?

Besides the free labor that the service-learners provide community agencies there are long-term benefits that service organizations receive from service-learners. This is because organizations have a vested interest in student learning. Students are members of their communities. As community members, whether communities are defined geographically or in some other way, students are both the clients and shareholders of community organizations. Service organizations in contemporary society are searching for interested and committed community members to help them realize their mission. Service-learning is one way in which service organizations can educate people about their missions and recruit their support.

Service organizations also realize that the act of participating in service can be tremendously satisfying. They know that students who serve and learn are more likely to establish long-term relationships with community service groups. Because of these factors, service organizations support service-learning as an important part of the educational process (Rocha, 2000; Teske & Brown, 2001).

As you can see, service-learning provides clear benefits for all those involved: students, teachers, colleges/universities, and communities. Service-learning is a classic win/win situation. All the parties receive some tangible benefit. While we do not claim that all parties obtain equal value from the experience, all involved satisfy some of their needs.

A word of caution, our experience with the world echoes that of Will Rogers who was fond of saying, "there ain't no such thing as a free lunch." We find this saying to be true of community service. While service-learning provides benefits for all parties involved, it requires commitment and work. While Chapter 2 discusses these kinds of issues in greater depth, we should make it clear in the beginning – service-learning does not require less work than other ways of learning. It is our opinion, however, that the benefits of service-learning far outweigh the effort required.

A NATURAL FIT WITH COMMUNICATION STUDIES

As communication students you may wonder what do I have to bring to a service placement? In a recent survey of community service professionals, the skills most in demand for volunteers or community service professionals were communication skills. Researchers (Brown et al, 2000) found that of the thirteen skills identified by community service professionals as most useful, the top two ranked skills involved communication. Overall, the study found that communication and conflict management skills were ranked as twice as important as any technical skill. A look at the want ads will confirm that communication skills are in demand. Ad after ad lists "good communication skills" as one of the most desirable characteristics for an applicant. As students of communication, your training in communication makes you a valuable asset to a service organization. These skills are so important that the National Communication Association is one of the nation's leaders in promoting and practicing service-learning.

The need for communication skills in community service is one aspect of the ideal fit between communication and service-learning. The second aspect is the universality of communication to the accomplishment of service. It does not matter where you chose to serve. Your primary skill will be your ability to communicate. This is true throughout the service sector. No matter what technical skill people in community service organizations use, their primary task is a communicative one.

SERVICE AS A CAREER

Another dimension of your service is the potential of your placement to develop into a career. Community service occupations are one of the fastest growing sectors of our economy. Due to changes in our society, contemporary Americans are less willing to devote their time to joining and managing non-profit and civic organizations (Brown et al, 2000; Wuthnow, 1998). This does not necessarily imply that Americans are now less concerned about their communities, only that the pattern of involvement is different. Americans now volunteer as much as ever, but the nature of their service activity has changed.

Americans are less willing to commit to long-term relationships with service organizations. While Americans are no longer making lifetime commitments to service organizations, they are increasingly willing to do episodic volunteering. Episodic volunteering is short term in nature. Volunteers tend to not take part in the planning or management of events; rather they arrive, "volunteer," and leave. This trend is also combined with the increase in giving to non-profit and community service organizations. The result of these trends is that service organizations now hire people to fill the roles committed volunteers once filled. This means that a clear career path for community service professionals has emerged.

Since communication skills are vital to success in community service, communication students are ideal candidates for community service jobs. The changes in how Americans express their concern for their communities have made community service a rapidly growing occupation. This author's institution now offers a community service major and degree to meet this demand. In summary, your service placement may also lead to a career in the emerging field of community service.

This chapter provides an introduction to the practice of service - learning. Throughout the rest of the book we will show you ways in which public communication is practiced in community service settings. Whether you are enrolled in a public speaking, persuasion, public relations, group or hybrid communication course, this text will help you to better understand and utilize the broad range of public communication techniques commonly employed in community service. Our aim is to help you achieve a positive service-learning experience, give you specific tools for becoming a more effective communicator in your community, and help you identify potential resources for your service. We hope as you learn more about service-learning you will share our enthusiasm and commitment to service while learning and be an active voice in our own community.

References

Brown K.J., Vande Sandt, L., Baney, P., Hauge, S., Lodge, A., Lodge, B., Lowendorf, V., McElligott, N., Racine, A., & Swingen, C. (2000). Montana State University-Northern Community Service research report. Paper presented at the Tools for Change Conference, Ellensburg, WA.

Campus Compact (1999). Introduction: A framework for service learning pedagogy. Campus Compact: introduction to service-learning institute. Providence: Brown University.

Campus Compact (1999). President's fourth of July declaration on responsibility in higher education. Campus Compact: introduction to service-learning institute. Providence: Brown University.

Ehrlich, T. (1996). In B. Jacoby et al. (eds.) <u>Service-learning in higher education: Concepts and practices</u>. San Francisco: Jossey-Bass.

Gray, M., Ondaatje, E. Fricker, R., & Geschwind, S. (2000). Assessing service-learning (the benefits of service-learning for students). <u>Change</u>, 32(2), 30-41.

Hepburn, M. (1997). Service learning in civic education: A concept with long, sturdy roots. <u>Theory Into Practice</u>, 36(3), 136-142.

Rocha, C. (2000). Evaluating experiential teaching methods in a policy practice course: The case for service-learning to increase political participation. <u>Journal of Social Work Education</u>, 36(11), 53-65.

Shumer, R. & Belbas, B. (1996). What we know about service-learning. <u>Education and Urban Society</u>, 28, 208-223.

Teske, A., & Brown, K.J. (2001). Getting a Head Start: The effect of mandatory volunteerism on the propensity to volunteer. Paper presented at the annual conference of the Northwest Communication Association, April 5-8, Cour D' Alene, ID.

Wuthnow, R. (1998). Loose connections: <u>Joining together in America's fragmented communities</u>. Cambridge: Harvard University Press.

Wutzdorff, A. & Giles, D. (1997). Service-learning in higher education. <u>Service-Learning</u>. Chicago: The National Society for Higher education.

CHAPTER 2

SERVICE-LEARNING MODELS

Now that you have an understanding of what service-learning involves, it will help to see which model for doing a service project your instructor has adopted. This chapter discusses the reasons for and against choosing to do a service project, rationales for required service-learning, the types of project you may undertake, and how you might identify a suitable service agency for the assignment if the you are required to do so. Your service assignment might be:
- Optional or required
- Direct, indirect or civic
- Designated by the instructor or your choice

WHEN SERVICE-LEARNING IS OPTIONAL

Most people like to have choices. We hope that if your instructor gives you a choice about whether or not to do service-learning for class credit you will choose this option. Service-learning may mean more work than traditional assignments, but feedback from students in our classes and research with more than 22,000 undergraduates (Astin, et. al., 2000) tells us that a service assignment also will yield more rewards.

Although the design of courses will vary from subject to subject and from instructor to instructor, here is an example of how the optional approach works.

Let's say you have enrolled in an interpersonal communication course. The final project for the class might be an assignment worth 30 percent of the total grade. The instructor might provide options such as:

1. Complete a 15-page research paper that summarizes, synthesizes and analyzes research literature on a fundamental theory of interpersonal communication.
2. Write a service-learning report that integrates interpersonal communication theory we have studied this semester with your work for a non-profit agency. You will be required to serve at least 15 hours, keep a journal of your experiences, and turn in a final paper of about 15 pages.

This represents only a thumbnail sketch of a possible assignment. Later pages of this chapter and others will flesh-out the details of typical service projects.

Because most students have written more than a few research papers, the familiar first option may seem more appealing. While the service option probably will be more challenging, it will pay off. As noted in chapter one, there are many reasons to choose service-learning. The benefits include:

- A more concrete understanding of the communication concepts and theories
- Professional enhancement and preparation for "the real world"
- A tangible, relevant accomplishment to put on your resume
- Personal growth through a challenging experience
- A chance to contribute to your community
- An opportunity to develop leadership skills
- Improved critical thinking ability
- Intangible rewards from helping others.

Student feedback in our classes supports these outcomes, as does a longitudinal national study (Astin, et. al., 2000) and other research (Cohen & Kinsey, 1994; Eyler, 1993; Kraft, 2000; Marcus, et. al., 1993). Here's a typical, anonymous student testimonial written as part of a course evaluation for an interpersonal communication course:

> *Going into this (service) project I had doubts that this was legit. Now I'm a believer. Doing rather than just reading helped me really understand what we studied in the book and class. I found myself actually using the stuff, and benefiting from it. My communication with people in many contexts has improved, and I get more of what we've been talking about in other comm classes as well as this one. The project made the theories, text and lectures real. I liked the idea of helping people and getting credit, but I had no idea that the (service) project would change my life. Thanks for giving us this opportunity.*

Consider the Requirements of Serving

Despite the benefits of a service project, you should think twice about this option. Not everyone should choose this assignment. Listed below are aspects of service-learning to consider when making your decision. This section also discusses ten important aspects of the project, such as contracts.

1. Beware of Overload

Some service -learning opportunities take more time to complete than a traditional project. If you have an 18-hour course load, work 20 or more hours per week at a job, serve as an officer of a student organization, regularly commute long distances, and have substantial family obligations, then a service project may push you over the edge this semester. It might be wise to pursue another option to save your sanity. There will be plenty of other opportunities to learn from service – though not necessarily for credit – during and after college. The people you work with and serve deserve your attention and energy. If you cannot give it, you do them a disfavor rather than a service.

2. Service-Learning Takes Time and Commitment

Your instructor may set a minimum number of hours for working with an agency or individual as part of the assignment. The time required can range from just a few hours for a minor assignment, to more than 40 hours during a 14 to 16-week semester. The weighting of the assignment often determines the hours required. For example, a Nonverbal Communication course taught at Winona State University included a service-learning project that determined a large portion of the final grade. That assignment required students to complete 30 hours of service between the third and 15th week of a 16-week semester. A less heavily weighted service project, such as writing a press release for a non-profit agency, might only require a few hours work. Alternative spring break service projects, such as those offered at Colorado State University, combine travel and a week of eight-hour days dedicated to service. Generally, you can count on putting in at least the minimum hours required for the project. However, in our experience we have found that many students find the experience so rewarding that they go above and beyond the call of the assignment, sometimes continuing their service and learning long after a class ends.

3. Contracts Put Your Commitment in Writing

Many professors and non-profit organizations require service-learners to sign contracts. Sometimes both will want your signature on different contracts. This practice promotes commitment and safety as well as clarifies what is expected of students. The instructor's contract often notes the project expectations, such as minimum hours of service, and lays out the objectives of the assignment. It may also clear the college or university of legal responsibility for your safety when you are off campus. Before signing a contract you may be required to set up an interview with a non-profit organization's representative. Your professor may ask you to get information about the site, the nature of clients served, and the services offered there, before having you sign a contract for the project. You should be aware that many instructors often ask for evidence of hours put in at the service site. This helps ensure that people who might be tempted to create a fictional account of service experience are not likely to do well on the project or in the class. Some instructors ask service agencies for reports on student's participation and performance, and the agency may have a sign-in sheet to document hours. Chapter 10 includes examples of different contracts used for service-learning assignments.

Before signing a contract with a service agency, a contact person with the organization may want you to come in for an interview. That interview may include questions about the objectives of your assignment as well as your motivation. Often you will also be asked what skills you have that might be put to use and to fill out a service schedule that indicates when you will be working for the agency. Service agencies use contracts to help cement your commitment. It will probably outline what is expected of you and serve as a legal document of your voluntary work status. Legal and safety problems related to service work are a concern because non-profit agencies, like all modern organizations, do need to protect their clients and themselves. Read any document carefully before signing it.

4. Learning by Reflecting, Writing and Synthesizing Does Not Come Easy

Service work often requires reading, critical thinking, and a considerable amount of writing. If you tend to put off writing, if you hate to write about your thoughts and feelings, if you don't like to think about how course concepts can be applied to your life, or if you're a hard core slacker, this project will prove difficult. Service projects entail reflection on your experiences and integration of course concepts with what you've seen and done. This proves easier if you keep up with your writing and check with the teacher to see if your insights about the application of theory and course concepts are correct. Waiting until the last minute to do the writing and reflecting usually proves disastrous. Synthesizing your experience with the theories explored in the text and lectures requires time and effort. Do not put off the academic learning until the last minute.

5. *Transportation Needs Can Complicate Service*

Some service projects can be done on campus, others cannot. Be sure you can get to and from the service site before making your decision. Clients will come to rely on you. Do not disappoint them by being a consistent no-show or late for appointments due to an inability to get to the site. If you do not have a car, but will need an automobile, you can often carpool with classmates working for the same client or agency. If you cannot be sure of reliable transportation you might want to opt out of the project.

6. *Maturity Matters*

Service-learning requires more personal responsibility than most other class projects. Service agencies need people they can count on. It helps to be a self-starter, someone who is motivated to work. You have to make a commitment to lend a hand and think critically about your service project. You have to pay close attention to your interaction with clients, noting what you can learn from them as well as your own behavior and thoughts. Not everyone is emotionally ready for this kind of work.

7. *Open Mindedness is Required*

While doing service work chances are you will be meeting people from a more diverse population than you normally encounter. You may be entering new territory. For this assignment to work you have to be open-minded to differences among both, agency co-workers and those you serve. Differences will include sexual orientation, religious beliefs, cultural expectations and norms, and a host of others. Do not be surprised if you find it uncomfortable, even a little scary, to work with people who may not share your background and beliefs. Most of us do at first. You may find yourself facing prejudices – your own and those of people you serve – of which you were not aware. If that is the case, then you will have lots to think about, discuss with classmates and your instructor, and to write about in your journal or final report on the project. If you cannot withhold judgement of your clients it is unlikely you will learn much from the assignment and that you will do them more harm than good.

8. Service-Learning is Neither Volunteering Nor Proselytizing

You do not earn credit for merely putting in hours with a non-profit or client. In other words, service-learning differs from volunteerism. This assignment requires you learn how to apply course concepts to your communication experiences with others, or to aid clients with your knowledge, skills, and attention. The emphasis of the assignment is on learning through service. You will be helping others, but they, by sharing their experiences, knowledge and opinions, and offering you the chance to practice your communication skills, will also be helping you. In fact, you may be the primary recipient of service from the project. Please keep in mind that you can learn much from people who may not have the social, educational, or economic advantages you have.

Also, remember that service is not missionary work. It might help to consider yourself to be a student abroad learning from others, not a missionary sent out to save others. Proselytizing, trying to convert others to your way of behaving, thinking, or believing is not the purpose of this project.

9. If in Doubt, Ask the Instructor

Teachers know that not everyone should do a service-learning project. Many instructors offer such assignments because they have seen how service-learning helps students effectively learn course material and grow in maturity and wisdom. Often the students who do not chose the service option regret their choice after hearing their peers report on experiences and insights. The vast majority of our students who undertake the service option report that the assignment proved to be one of the high points of their college career. If you have the service-learning option, give it serious consideration. If you need help making up your mind, consult your instructor about your concerns and ask for her, or his, feedback. Your professor can help you make the best choice.

10. A Short-term Project Can Become Long-term

There is one more thing you should consider when making your choice. What starts as a short-term project may become a long-term commitment. Service projects seldom last more than the length of a course. However, you may find yourself staying with a service agency or client long after the term has ended. What begins as a class project may become a part of your life and identity. People who do service work frequently conclude they get more from helping others than they give. For example, a woman attending the University of Missouri began working in a soup kitchen as part of a sociology class requirement. When the semester ended she stayed on. She worked Sunday evenings at the kitchen for more than two years until graduating and moving on, and she regarded the job as one of the richest parts of her education (Dorries, 1995). Doing a research paper or delivering a speech is relatively predictable. But you never know exactly what the future may hold when you sign up for service-learning.

WHEN SERVICE-LEARNING IS REQUIRED

To paraphrase Evenus, a Greek philosopher, "Compulsory course assignments are bitterness to the soul." For some students doing service-learning seems more like a burden than an opportunity. We believe, and hope you will come to see, that service projects enlighten individuals and lightens learning. However, you may be skeptical. You may have questions, such as: "Why is (*your instructor's name here*) making us do a service project? This isn't like my other class assignments and I don't see the connection to the course. Isn't this just a pet project to support the professor's political agenda?" You may feel some resentment about having to do work that is not a traditional assignment for a college class. You may feel like you are being forced to do good against your will. Here are some straight answers to these questions and concerns.

Research about service projects indicates that students, faculty, and communication departments all benefit from this approach to learning. The purpose of service-learning is learning – to enhance and advance your education. Many people mistakenly think that service-learning is forced volunteerism for a cause. Although service-learning requires students to apply knowledge in a way that helps others, it is not politically driven. Service to others transcends political ideology. It may help you to know that many colleges and universities now require service work as an increasingly vital element of education for adult citizens of a democratic society (Astin, et. al., 2000; Droge & Murphy, 1999; Kraft, 2000).

Service work is also increasingly a typical part of working for modern organizations. Businesses, industry, and government agencies seek to hire people who willingly give time and energy to the communities in which they live and work. In many organizations doing service for the community is a de facto part of work, though it may not be written into job descriptions. The payoff is not only good public relations for the organization, it also teaches workers the importance of involvement with the local community (Hendrix, 2001). Employees learn about the lives of the people who they serve and have a better understanding of the problems of their community. The same is true for classroom assignments. You learn about real people and their real problems and often you get to offer solutions based on your learning that can help them (Markus, et. al., 1993).

Still, you may want more evidence of what you will receive from required service-learning. Here are some of the reasons why your instructor may have chosen to require a service project that you may not have considered:

Service-Learning Offers Practical Experience

Working outside of the classroom will require you to develop problem-solving abilities based on your learning. You will find that as you help others in need of assistance, you will have to use the knowledge discussed in texts and lectures. Service-learning makes textbook and lecture material more real, more concrete. Service projects combine your experiences with learning course content in a purposeful way.

Service Projects Force People Out of Their Comfort Zones

Some of us need an incentive to expand the comfortable "bubbles" we create around our lives. Leaving our comfort zone almost always enlarges our knowledge and understanding of the world. College is about growth; from service-learning we often have to reach beyond our previous boundaries. Service projects introduce students to the larger community and the issues that affect others. Often they require us to interact with strangers, leaving the security of the known. Just as public speaking courses require people to face fears in order to grow, service-learning helps students overcome apprehension about entering an unfamiliar community, as well as to confront the injustices and unfairness of society. Service-learning can lead to personal insight, public action, and greater participation in the democratic processes.

Service-learning Encourages Leadership

Some students feel they do not have much to offer clients. They do not realize they can provide useful information and skills, attention through individual care, excitement (especially for the children and the elderly), and friendship. For young people you can offer support, help them set goals, and provide a role model of a socially successful adult. Student volunteers often mentor others, especially when they work with children, teenagers, and immigrants. Service provides a chance to practice sharing your knowledge and experience for the benefit of others. That's leadership. Working in groups on service presentations also requires leadership.

Service Builds Teamwork Skills

Many times you and your classmates may be working for the same agency, sometimes with the same clients. You may also be working with representatives of service organizations or with government employees. Such projects require effective group communication and teamwork skills. Most modern organizations require just such experience and know-how.

Service Nurtures Responsibility, Empathy, and Altruism

Service projects allow students the opportunity to see life from another person's perspective. Often that point of view is more privileged than that of many college students. Helping people tends to increase awareness of, and appreciation of, others and their concerns. A college education should be more than training for a job. It should help you become a better human being. Service-learning helps make this part of your education possible.

Service Promotes Democracy

Service-learning emphasizes good citizenship and an ethic of service, both of which are fundamental to the success of our political and social processes. But you may still have your doubts about the value of service-learning. Most instructors welcome your questions. Share your doubts and concerns with your teacher. When students in our classes express skepticism about service-learning we try to explain our reasons for requiring the project. If a student respectfully disagrees with the nature of the assignment and explains why he or she objects to service-learning, we offer them a more traditional project. It is likely your teacher will do the same. Finally, here are a few sample comments from students who we obligated to complete a service-learning assignment:

> *I must say that the service-learning portion of the class was a surprise, unwelcome at first, then pleasantly surprising. The service-learning activities I have experienced throughout this class have affected my life in ways I never would have imagined. I feel that, through this experience, I have learned more about myself this month than I have in the past three years.*
> *"[Service-learning] has helped me broaden my horizons in a way that will affect me for the rest of my life."*

"Service-learning should be a part of every person's life. Not only do the people you are serving benefit, from you as a volunteer will benefit greatly as well"

"Because of the service-learning component of this course, I now know that I am going to quit saying 'I should get more involved and do some community service. Now I actually will.' 'I think that I will have a greater tendency to give of myself.'"

"I think of the service-learning component as a gift I received from this class."

THREE TYPES OF SERVICE: DIRECT, INDIRECT, AND CIVIC

Usually your service will be direct, indirect, or civic in nature. Direct, indirect, and civic service projects involve different types of work and learning. Knowing which type you will be undertaking helps you to understand and take on the assignment.

Direct service involves working face-to-face with people in need. You get immediate feedback about your efforts from the people you serve. However, it can also be very demanding. Examples include students of interpersonal communication who visit weekly with elderly residents of a full-care facility, and intercultural communication students who aid immigrants by explaining what to buy at the local grocery stores or how to study for a driver's license test. This type of service can be especially rewarding because you see first-hand how your work benefits others and nurtures friendships.

One downside of this type of service occurs when the project concludes. Although some students continue to work with their clients, most end the relationship when the class concludes. That can be disappointing and painful for the people you serve, especially children, even if they know you have been helping them as part of a class project. It takes diplomacy and tact to exit a relationship with a client who has come to see you as an aid or friend. In general, we advise our students to emphasize – from the start of a service project and throughout the term – the temporary nature of their commitment. It helps to repeatedly tell people you serve what you hope to gain from the experience and, in some cases, why you will not be able to continue to meet them when the semester ends. It is more ethical to be open and honest about your limited commitment than to build false expectations. Leaving children proves especially heart wrenching. It helps to discuss strategies for how you will exit the service setting with professionals who work with an agency. It also proves a useful topic for classroom discussions.

Indirect service usually entails providing a service, product, or report, for a non-profit agency that helps others. While you may not directly assist clients, your efforts do support the organization which aids others in the community. Oftentimes indirect service includes counseling a non-profit agency about their communication practices. One example includes a group of students in a public relations campaigns class at Radford University who suggested, and later created, materials to promote awareness and financial support for a women's shelter. Another group of students created a membership survey for a local chamber of commerce to help the organization maintain and increase membership. This type of service often provides you with material that can be included in portfolios. For example, Beth Mickey, a Communication student at Radford, used her newsletter and press releases created for a county child welfare agency as writing samples in an application for a job she landed with a children's museum.

Civic service usually supports a social cause or addresses a community issue. This type of project may include working with government agencies or social movement organizations. It may include challenging powerful institutions, seeking to right social injustices or unfairness. For example, students in a political communication course might establish a voter registration campaign in their community to help empower minority groups. Students in an introduction to communication class at Winona State University organized and carried out a clean-up campaign of a wildlife area, and group communication students at Colorado State University did the same for a city park.

No matter which of these approaches your assignment requires, direct, indirect, or civic, the service will touch the lives of others while providing you with concrete experiences to improve your communication skills and to analyze and learn course concepts. Developing a connection with a service agency may also prove to be one element of the assignment.

FINDING A SERVICE PROJECT SITE

Although many instructors line-up non-profit agencies for service projects before a class begins, others let students do this work as part of the assignment. This is not just laziness on their part. Having students, individually, or in groups, find, choose, and contact these organizations can be a significant part of learning. It may require teamwork, research, critical thinking, and considerable communication with agencies before you find the right fit. Communication student's choices for service projects also can prove very creative.

Students often have a lot to say in their project reports about the agencies they counsel or that link them to clients. Often they write critically about the communication competence of their contacts, or lack thereof, comparing service organization staff's behavior to models, concepts, and theories from class. It is important to remember that many non-profits do not have the financial or staff resources to communicate "by the book."

If you, or your group, have been charged with finding a service organization, you will need some direction. Your instructor probably has some advice, and maybe a handout, to help you get started. You may be given a list of service agencies with the names of contact persons, phone numbers, addresses, etc. from which to choose. What follows are questions to ask as you go about finding a service agency suitable for your assignment.

Can you fulfill the assignment and fit the needs of the client? Re-read the assignment. Knowing what you've been asked to do will help you eliminate many service possibilities that would not be suitable for the project and course objectives.

Will the organization or client be suitable for you or your group? Do you find the organization appealing? Does the client, or staff of the organization appear willing to work with you? Are they enthusiastic about your inquiry? Is the contact person you will be working with cooperative and interested in your inquiry? Does he or she understand the assignment after you explain it to them, and is she or he willing to help you meet the goals of the project? What about your own thoughts and feelings about working with a service organization? Your sense of connection and enthusiasm matters – if you haven't got any for a particular agency or for the people you will serve, pursue another option.

Is there a campus office that helps connect students with service agencies? Some colleges have staff who coordinate service-learning and community volunteerism. Alternatively, you can try contacting the local office of the United Way. This non-profit agency often has lists of service providers looking for people who can help.

Do you (or does someone in your group) already provide service to an organization in the community or on campus? Could this agency work with you on this assignment? These can include synagogues, churches, temples, and mosques, as well as secular service agencies. Having a previous, successful relationship with an organization can make for a smoother project.

Is there a social issue of special concern to you? What do you worry about? Service motivated by your own feelings and commitment tends to increase the likeliness of a good fit and success.

Finally, if your entire class is working on one project it may require a lot of planning to accommodate everyone and their different schedules. Very few service organizations need 20 or more volunteers at the same time. In this case, you may want to create a project, such as a special fundraiser or one-time campaign, for the class to undertake.

REFERENCES

Astin, A., Vogelgesang, L., Ikeda, E. & Yee, J. (date). How Service-Learning Affects Students [On-line}. Available www.eseis.ucla.edu/slc/Research.html

Cohen, J. & Kinsey, D. (1994). Doing good and scholarship: A service-learning study. Journalism Educator. Winter, 4-14.

Dorries, B. (1995). Soup Kitchen Stories: The Dialectic of Service. An unpublished dissertation, University of Missouri.

Droge, D. & Murphy, B. (1999). Voices of Strong Democracy Concepts and Models for Service-Learning in Communication Studies. American Association of Higher Education, Washington, D.C.

Eyler, J. (1993). Comparing the impact of two internship experiences on student learning. Journal of Cooperative Education. Fall, 41-52.

Hendrix, K. (2001). Public relations cases (5th ed.). Belmont, CA: Wadsworth.

Kraft, N. (2000). The role of service-learning in critical thinking. In D. Weil & H.K. Anderson (Eds.), Perspectives in critical thinking: Essays by teachers in theory and practice. (pp. 75-94). New York: Peter Lang.

Markus, G., Howard, J., & King, D. (1993). Integrating community service-learning and classroom instruction enhances learning: Results from an experiment. <u>Education Evaluation and Policy Analysis,</u> 15, 410-419.

CHAPTER 3

ACHIEVING A POSITIVE SERVICE-LEARNING EXPERIENCE

Now that you have an idea about the history and different types of service-learning engagements, it is time to discuss how to have a positive service-learning experience. Much of the responsibility for having a positive service-learning experience rests upon whoever arranges for the service placement. As discussed in the previous chapter, you may be the one who arranges for the placement. If your instructor has arranged for the placement, you will be asked to report back about the adequacy and appropriateness of the placement. So, how do you find a good match between a service agency and yourself? The first step is assessing the fit between your goals and skills, and the needs of a service placement.

MATCHING STUDENT GOALS AND SKILLS WITH A SERVICE AGENCY

As you have read in Chapter 2, one of the most important aspects of any service-learning project is the match between the student, the project, and the agency. In the best service-learning experiences the needs of all the parties are satisfied. Much of the satisfaction in a service project comes from the fit between the student, the project, and the nature of the agency.

It is important to find a service engagement that allows you to fulfill your learning goals and use the skills you are acquiring through course study. The first step in this process is gaining a clear understanding of the instructor's goals of the course. The second step in this process is to determine, in conjunction with your instructor, your goals for the course. The third step is to assess your course and service-learning goals in relation to those of the agency.

Selecting a Service Agency to Fulfill Course Goals

Instructors usually outline course goals and course descriptions in the syllabus or at the beginning of the course. Course goals typically come in two types: skill and theoretical goals. A skills-based learning goal is a course goal that focuses on developing and using a specific set of skills. Skills-based learning goals usually look something like this example from a public relations course:

Example 3.1

> *Course Goals: This course should prepare students to consume and produce public relations. Students will produce public relations materials such as press releases, press kits, brochures, and internal reports. This course is focused on the practical accomplishment of their understandings of the nature and skills of public relations.*

As you can see in this example, the focus is on developing and practicing a specific set of skills, in this case, the production of press releases, press kits, brochures and internal reports. Typically in skills-based service-learning courses, evaluation and service activities focus on developing and practicing a specific set of skills. Courses that focus on skill development often will use a portfolio system to track your progress and accomplishment. In skills-based courses service placements and the reflection that is a part of service-learning will revolve around these skills. In contrast, theoretically focused courses typically ask you to focus on the ideas presented in the course rather than on the practice of a specific set of skills. An example of this sort is the course goal for an interviewing course shown here:

Example 3.2

> *Course Goal: The development of an understanding of interviews through discussion and examination of the interview process. A theoretical basis for interviewing will be the emphasis for discussion. This examination is based within the transactional, negotiated, and common meaning of the interview.*

As this example illustrates, a course can be, especially one traditionally taught, oriented towards theory. Traditionally, an instructor will ask you to focus on understanding theory rather than on the application of skills. In theoretically based courses the class discussion, evaluation, and reflection is centered on using the service to illustrate and deepen the theories and insights taught in the course. However, it is possible to choose to focus on both theoretical understanding and practical accomplishment. One of the strengths of service-learning is that it allows you to focus on both theory and application. The course below illustrates how this is described for a small group communication course.

Example 3.3

Course Goals

This course should prepare students to participate in, and lead small groups. To do this proficiently, students should gain an understanding of the nature and role of groups in human society. This understanding requires both theoretical understanding and practical accomplishment. In light of this, the goals of this course are two-fold: first, theoretical understanding of group process, and second, practical accomplishment of those understandings.

This course asks you to focus on both the theory and its application. While this may seem like more work than a class that focuses exclusively on a single type of understanding, it offers you a chance to gain much more than you would from a course with a single orientation. Many service-learning courses will ask you to focus on both theory and application. Once you determine the course goals you can start trying to match opportunities for service with your course goals.

The next step in this process is to decide what you hope to accomplish in the course. While this may seem trite, "I want an A," is a reply we often hear initially; we encourage you to move beyond the obvious outcome measures, such as grades, and reflect on what is valuable about your university or college experience. One of the things service-learning offers is an opportunity to direct your own education. By thinking carefully about what you hope to learn through your service and coursework, you have an opportunity to tailor your education to your needs. One student expressed the idea like this in her reflection journal:

Example 3.4

> *...it was really tough at first to work there, I didn't want to go in sometimes because it was so depressing, but after while it was the kids and the relationships that drew me into it. After while I stopped seeing the kids as victims and dependent and just as kids. I learned*

30

that they were so tough and even though I hurt for them they didn't cry for themselves. That was an important lesson for me. I'm glad I chose to work there though or I would never have known the kids or understood where they come from and I think that I even understand myself better now.

As you can see in this example, thinking carefully about a choice of a service placement directly influences the nature of your learning. It is essential you choose a community partner to work with that will allow you to fulfill the stated and required learning goals of a course. If you have to write press releases and brochures for a community partner as required in the public relations syllabus in Example 3.1, then it is essential to pick a community partner that will allow you to do those things. Up to this point we have been talking about choosing a service agency for what they can do for you. It is also important to consider what you can do for the agency in choosing a service placement

ALIGNING SERVICE-LEARNING GOALS WITH AGENCY GOALS

As important as it is to assess and find a good fit between the course and student needs and what a community partner offers, it is equally as important to ensure a fit between the community partner's needs and the student's skills. The general idea behind any sort of service is that the agency should receive at least as much as give. While this may seem anti-intuitive –"of course we give a lot to any partner, we are doing service." The community partners have reported that "volunteers" are sometimes more trouble to supervise, manage, and integrate into their operation than the little they contributed to the goal of the organization. We have both an ethical and functional responsibility to contribute to the overall mission of the community partner in tangible and substantial ways.

Another issue for both the community partners and service-learning students is the issue of satisfaction with the experience. Recent research has indicated that satisfaction for volunteers results from two factors: the degree to which volunteers perceive that their activities contributed to the goal of the organization, and the degree to which volunteers feel other members of the organization treat them as partners in accomplishing those organizational goals. This illustrates that placements featuring meaningful tasks accomplished by students with the skills to undertake them are the most successful and satisfying service relationships. This means that you need to spend time with a potential community partner figuring out what they need from you and what skills you bring to the table.

In this process it is important to keep two things in mind. First, you can do more than you think you can, and second, by the nature of your course work you may find you have skills you did not know were in demand. In reality, college students often possess skills and abilities that are in demand in service organizations.

A word of warning however, at a recent conference on service-learning this author attended, the question was asked, "what skills do you need to bring to a service placement?" Most of the students answered "empathy." While empathy is a valuable trait, it was not on the list of attributes that most non-profit and governmental entities (potential placements) seek in a volunteer. In a recent survey of potential placement agencies, the skills that were ranked the highest were conflict skills, communication skills, and dependability. At a lower level, computer, accounting, and writing skills were also seen as valuable (see Example 3.5).

Example 3.5

Conflict skills	**4.8**
Communication	**4.7**
Dependability	**4.2**
Accounting	**3.1**
Computer skills	**2.5**
General writing skills	**2.2**

Community service skills

As you can see from these ratings, the skills communication students should possess are in demand in service organizations. Beyond the general skills identified in this study, most service placements will have specific tasks they wish to have performed that require students to apply skills they learn in class. At times service organizations will be unsure as to the role you will be performing. Beware of committing to doing "whatever." While you should be open and responsive to the needs of the organization, the most productive service relationships are those in which both parties have clear expectations. A preliminary meeting in which you discuss your role with the organization is a good idea. When talking to a potential agency about your role in the organization it is good to keep in mind the requirements for serving outlined in Chapter 2.

- Beware of overload
- A short term project can become long term
- Service-learning takes time and commitment
- Transportation needs complicate service
- Open mindedness is required
- Service-learning is neither volunteering nor proselytizing

The bottom line is simple – finding a service placement that allows you to exercise your skills to help the organization accomplish its goals usually will result in a positive service-learning experience. The next step after you have found a service placement and negotiated your role with the organization is beginning service. Having a positive service-learning experience will depend largely on the attitude with which you approach your service.

CULTIVATING A PROFESSIONAL ATTITUDE

How you approach your service is at least as important as where you serve. Your attitude towards your service can determine what kind of experience you have and your relationship with others in your organization. There are two attitude traps that students sometimes fall into in their service. These traps involve how students view the nature of their engagement with the service organization.

The Charity Trap
The charity trap is based on a particular conception of what community service is about. In this trap, service-learners view themselves as engaged in charity. Charity is often seen, as one student put it, as "helping the poor." If students go into a placement with the attitude that they are going to "help those poor people," they almost invariably encounter difficulties. First, it is demeaning and paternalistic to refer to, and treat people as "those poor people." Both, workers in the service agency and its clients are sure to resist that kind of characterization. Second, this attitude builds a sense of superiority that is visible to the people you work with. This emphasizes the difference between students and others and reinforces the idea that their condition is a permanent trait. The second trap is like the charity trap but slightly different in focus. It is the health trap.

The Health Trap

The health trap, like the charity trap, is about attitude. This trap is based upon viewing service from a health metaphor. With this attitude, servers view themselves as health professionals who are in service to cure individuals. There are several problems with this attitude. The first comes from viewing others as, "sick" and you as, "well." This is an insulting, and all too often, visible attitude that usually offends those being served. It also has the potential to offend those who are currently in service since there is an underlying assumption inherent in this attitude that the previous "physician" failed. Those who have been previously, and often professionally, in service, often perceive this attitude as arrogance and naiveté. The second problem with this attitude is that it assumes that the condition generating the need for service can, like a disease, be treated and cured by the application of some sort of technology. This assumption causes problems, since it is based upon the belief that the individuals and/or the organization are incapable of "curing" themselves without the service learner. While good service placements allow servers to bring their skills to bear on a problem, it is rare to find a placement where a student "cures" poverty or any other social issue. Through reflecting on her experience, one student came to realize that she had fallen into these traps. She wrote in her journal:

> *I realize now that I expected to go into the school and solve all the kids "problems." Like I was their savior or something. When they didn't welcome me with trumpets and gratitude I felt like they were ungrateful, and when I couldn't solve all their problems I felt like I had failed. I realize now after we talked about the charity trap and the health trap in class that that was me. I expected to come into the school and solve all the problems like the teachers, parents, and even the kids didn't know what they were doing. Because I was a community service student I could cure everyone.*

The key to avoiding these attitude traps is to develop a professional attitude.

THE STEPS TO GAINING A PROFESSIONAL ATTITUDE

To gain the proper attitude for service it is useful to think of yourself as a person committed to performing a task for an organization. In some ways it is similar to taking a job. From the organizational viewpoint they are investing in you just as they would any organizational member. Think of yourself as being compensated for your efforts. Besides the satisfaction you will derive from a positive service-learning experience, you will also be compensated in your class for your efforts. Whether your service-learning is mandatory or serves as an optional part of the class, completing your commitment fulfills some of your course responsibilities. In a sense, you are working for compensation – credits. You are a professional. We are encouraging you to embrace a professional attitude toward your placement.

As discussed in Chapter 2, service-learning takes commitment from the both parties involved in the service. You commit time, effort, and talent. The organization commits resources to train you, manage your work, and monitor your impact on the organization's mission. The first aspect of professionalism is time management.

1. Budgeting Time

One of the great challenges of a college student's life is time management. There never seems to be enough time to get done all the things you want to do in a day. People in the professional world feel these same time pressures. Look in almost any airport bookstore and you will find it filled with time management books trumpeting their place on the various bestseller lists. Time matters; your time matters, the organization's time matters, and for the people being served, time matters. Professionals must organize and track their time. There are several suggestions we can offer about budgeting your time.

Many placements will require you to direct activities. Failing to budget your time adequately and arriving late reflects badly on you, but just as importantly, your supervisor also looks bad and the program participants are disappointed and frustrated. Plan for necessary travel time and factor traffic or weather conditions. While service-learning offers unique opportunities for learning, serving demands that you schedule time to accomplish it just as you would for any class. When you skip or rearrange homework time, it carries negative consequences. When you miss or arrive late for a service-learning assignment others suffer the consequences. We know it will be tempting to occasionally rearrange or miss your service commitment. While in some placements this is not a problem, in others it will be an immediate problem. Just as missing class and putting off homework may lead to lower grades, even academic failure, these habits foster negative service relationships for both the student and service organization.

Time constraints should be one of the topics in your initial interview. It is important that you realistically represent to the agency the time you can commit. You should calculate available time and allocate a realistic amount to your service engagement. If you treat your commitment to service-learning as a priority and honor your commitments to the service organization, you will find the time you spend serving will be a positive experience.

2. Meeting Agency Expectations

A second and equally important area that contributes to a professional attitude is your commitment to meeting agency expectations. In your initial interview it is essential that you gain a clear understanding of what the service organization expects from you. This should be part of the give and take when you communicate your expectations and the agency offers theirs. Often this conversation will be supplemented or summarized in a written contract. Some service organizations will have standard contracts for service workers. If they do, it is still essential to sit down with your supervisor and make certain your have a shared understanding about your time and resource commitment.

Discovering a service organization's expectations is the first step in meeting their expectations. In this process it is important to realize that you are, albeit temporarily, a member of the organization. As a member you have an obligation to contribute to the goal of the organization. In the initial interview it is critical that you understand what they expect from you. Typically, organizations, especially those with experience with service-learners, will articulate clear task expectations. Agencies assume your loyalty, dependability, and trustworthiness. Organizations are not interested in having members who openly criticize co-workers, arrive late, miss work, refuse or fail to perform tasks, or denigrate the organization in public. Service organizations expect you to act as would any organizational member. After you have budgeted and committed your time and learned the organization's expectations, the third step to developing a professional attitude is to prepare yourself to work in a challenging communication environment.

3. *Working in a Challenging Communication Environment*

As communication students you should be aware of the special demands of communication. This is particularly true when we enter new work or social environments. Service organizations are particularly complex and difficult sites for communication. For example, one student chose to work for a domestic abuse hotline. During her service she had to interact with a great variety of people in various roles. As a member of the hotline staff she interacted with clients, other staffers, her supervisor, other Human Resource Development Agency (HRDC) workers, and community members. She was faced with the challenge of figuring out her relationship and communication style for all of these engagements.

Fortunately, those who work in the field recognize the challenge of communication in this environment. When asked what skills are important for volunteers, community service professionals identified communication and conflict skills as the two top areas. This is illustrated in Example 3.5.

One factor that makes communication challenging is the transitory nature of many people's engagement with service organizations. Many service organizations feature a work force made up of mostly volunteers surrounding a core of committed organizational members. Add to this fact the reality that many service organizations provide services for relatively short periods of time. This means that many people you encounter are still learning how to effectively work within the organization. Long-term relationships and the ensuing communication familiarity and ease that result are rare. A good comparison is to contrast your comfort with long time friends, to how you feel around people you have just met or with whom you work. This makes communicating a challenge.

The diversity of service organizations also offers a communication challenge. Most service organizations have a variety of people performing a variety of roles. It is not unusual to have volunteers, employees, and clients all working together on the same project. In contrast, typical business organizations have paid employees and paying customers who interact in clearly defined hierarchies. This lack of division of tasks and clear hierarchies, while in many ways refreshing, may lead to confusion about relationships between people and about proper attitudes of address and communication. The example of the domestic abuse hotline we talked about earlier illustrates this kind of complexity. In this kind of situation it is easy for a casual comment to offend. A good rule of thumb is to treat all people with respect and to remember that as a communication practitioner you need to take the responsibility for being sensitive to other's communicative attitudes. Another factor that makes communication in service organizations challenging is the diversity of experience and backgrounds you are likely to encounter.

WORKING WITH DIVERSE POPULATIONS

You may encounter a diverse group of people in your service placement as far as organizational role and commitment. There are many other areas in which the diversity you encounter may present a communication challenge. Communicating with people with whom you have little experience can be challenging. It becomes even more challenging when the person with whom you are communicating is significantly different from you. Adopting a professional attitude towards your service placement means taking the responsibility to adjust your communication to the context.

Dealing with Difference
Age is one way in which people may differ from you in your service-learning placement. You may choose to work with children, teenagers, adults, or seniors, but at times interact with people from all these age groups to accomplish your goals. Whatever your age, race, sexual orientation, or abilities, you are sure to encounter people who differ significantly from you in one or more of these categories. College can be an insular experience. Most of us tend to spend the majority of our time interacting with those like ourselves. Consequently, we often have little practice in communicating with differing people or groups.

The prospect of communicating with people that differ from you in age, race, ethnicity, physical abilities, or sexual orientation may seem daunting. Remember that if you are sensitive to how they communicate and accept responsibility for the conversation's success, communicating with people of different ages and backgrounds can be a positive experience. You may be impressed by the similarities you share with people who differ from you. At other times you may gain insight into yourself and others by focusing on your differences. Either way, if you focus on learning as you serve, encountering people different from you should be a positive learning experience. Remember that an essential part of any service experience is using differences to reflect on your own values and communication style.

COMMON STUDENT QUESTIONS

At this point we are sure you have questions. In this section we will attempt to anticipate your questions by answering some of the frequently asked questions that students have asked us in our service-learning courses.

Question 1 – *How do I find a group to work with?*

The answer to this question depends upon your interests and abilities. The first step is to decide what interests you. Do you like to work with kids? Seniors? Horses? Do you enjoy sports? Do you like to read? Do you have any special skills? Music? Sports? Art? Any of these areas could be the start. The second step is to find out what organizations need help in the area. Most community service organizations will be eager to welcome your contribution. Your instructor may have a list of organizations looking for service-learners. A local community resource directory is also a good place to start. The key is to sit down with your available options and reflect on your interests and abilities and try to find a match.

Question 2 – *How do I know I will pick the right organization?*

The answer is easy – you won't. However, careful consideration of your abilities and interests should enable you to find an organization that is right for you. A key in this process is the initial interview. In that interview be sure to ask about supervision, responsibilities, and time commitments. A good interview will enable you to make sure, as much as possible, that you are a good fit with the organization. In the end though, you will learn as much, or more from a difficult placement as from an easy one.

Question 3 – *What if I get in over my head?*

If you feel that you are in over your head you have two resources – your instructor and your supervisor. Talk to your instructor about your situation. Instructors can often help you manage the problem. Your supervisor can also help in these situations. Remember, communication is the key. You, your supervisor, and your instructor all have an interest in your success. But they cannot help you with a problem they do not know about. One way to prevent this from happening is to develop a written service contract with the organization that outlines your duties and responsibilities in advance.

<u>Question 4</u> – *Why won't they let me do _____?*

Most service organizations have restrictions about the activities in which a service learner can engage. These restrictions are put in place to protect the agency, their clients, and the service learner. It is a good idea to ask about these sorts of restrictions in your initial interview.

<u>Question 5</u> – *What if they want more than I am willing to give?*

Again, the key to this issue is communication and an adequate understanding of your service placement. Starting with the initial interview and a written contract, it is incumbent upon you to act professionally. Part of this responsibility is to notify your instructor or supervisor if you are asked to perform tasks with which you are uncomfortable. If the organization asks you to commit more time or accept responsibilities that you are unprepared to accept, it is your responsibility to speak up. This holds true even if you are aware of the organization's need. Remember communication is the key.

<u>Question 6</u> – *Why aren't they more organized?*

It is easy to forget, as a person who comes into an organization for a few hours a week, that the organization does not revolve around your activities. You should expect to be a low priority at times. You may not get your phone calls returned as quickly as you would like, or find everything ready to go when you arrive. Many service organizations are chronically under-funded, under-staffed, and under-appreciated. As a consequence, they seek volunteers, and you, service-learners, to help. This author recently took a group of volunteers to work at a local food bank. The volunteers made numerous comments about the inadequacies of the organization. When someone suggested that the food bank could use the help of people who perceived the problem so acutely, the room fell silent and no one stepped forward to volunteer resolutions. Try to maintain a professional attitude and contribute more than you demand.

<u>Question 7</u> – *How can I just walk away?*

Many placements confront service-learners with emotionally demanding situations. The answer to how to walk away is in two parts. The first part is that you don't have to walk away. If by serving you learn that there is an unmet community need that moves you, then a service placement can begin your long-term commitment to serve that need. The second part of the answer is to rely on your instructor and supervisor to help you contextualize your experiences. Another key is to write about your issues.

The reflective writing component of your service should be a place where you work through the issues you encounter as you serve.

Summary

In summary, it is important to remember that having a successful service-learning experience depends upon your attitude, the match between your goals and skills and the agency's expectations, and your adaptability as a communicator. It is also important to rely on the advice of your instructor and of your contact with the agency to help you accomplish your goals. Any problems or obstacles you encounter can usually be overcome if you immediately take the initiative to discuss them with either your instructor or your agency contact. Finally, we have talked about the commitment and effort that is required by service-learning. However, we feel that the rewards far outweigh the costs.

REFERENCES

Battistoni, R.M. (2000). Service learning in political science: An introduction. PS: Political Science and Politics 33(3), 615-617.

Brown K.J., Vande Sandt, L., Baney, P., Hauge, S., Lodge, A., Lodge, B., Lowendorf, V., McElligott, N., Racine, A., & Swingen, C. (2000). Montana State University-Northern Community Service research report. Paper presented at the Tools for Change Conference, Ellensburg, WA.

Carpini, M.X. & Keeter, S. (2000). What should be learned through Service learning? PS: Political Science and Politics 33(3), 635-641.

Chapin, J.R. (1998). Is service learning a good idea? Data from the national longitudinal study of 1988. The Social Studies, 89(5), 205-214.

Dionne, E. (1998). Community works: The revival of civil society in America. Washington, D.C.: The Brookings Institute.

Du Bois, W.E. &, Lappe, F. (1994). The quickening of America: Rebuilding our nation, remaking our lives. San Francisco, CA: Jossey-Bass Inc.

Gray, J.G., Ondaatje, E.H., Fricker, R.D., & Geshwind, S.A. (2000). Assessing service learning. <u>Change 32</u>(2), 30-42.

Hunter, S. & Brisbin, R.A. (2000). The impact of service learning on democratic and civic values. <u>PS: Political Science and Politics 33</u>(3), 623-631.

Kahne, J. and Westheimer, J. (1996, May). In the service of what: The politics of service learning. <u>Phi Delta Kappan</u>, 593-599.

Kielsmeier, J.C. (2000). A time to serve, a time to learn – service learning and the promise of democracy. <u>Phi Delta Kappan 81</u>(9), 652-660.

MacNeil, C. and Krensky, B. (1996). A project yes case study: Who are the real service providers? <u>Education and Urban Society, 28</u>(2), 176-188.

Rocha, C.J. (2000). Evaluating experiential teaching methods in a policy practice course: The case for service learning to increase political participation. <u>Journal of Social Work Education, 36</u>(1), 53-64.

Rowls, M. & Swick, K.J. (2000). Designing teacher education course syllabi that integrate service learning. <u>Journal of instructional Psychology 27</u>(3), 187-199.

CHAPTER 4

DESIGNING INFORMATIVE SERVICE-LEARNING PRESENTATIONS

After students have completed most or all of their volunteer assignments, I assign an informational service-learning speech. Videotaping these presentations allows students to transcend the immediate course, becoming part of a service-learning archive for future use. This library of speeches fits the value-added model of service-learning, providing others with a tutorial on the demands, rewards, and applications of service-learning from a student's perspective. These speeches cover recommendations for volunteer placements, descriptions of requirements and agency expectations, logistical demands, and personal career and community benefits. Viewing these taped speeches early in the semester provides a blueprint for optimal benefit from the service experience and as an incentive for community involvement. An informative speech can change attitudes and illustrate how informative and persuasive discourse sometimes overlaps. Beyond the benefit to other students, speakers who choose a service subject often deliver their best speeches, as they speak from direct experience. Imparting the do's and don'ts or rewards of a service-learning experience also creates an array of meaningful subjects for an informative presentation. The summarized speech that follows, "Building Your Career through Service-Learning," provides one such example.

A speech directed at career development is guaranteed to interest a college audience. This speaker established credibility by citing respected business analyst Marshall Loeb's view that a well chosen volunteer experience creates marketable job skills, including event planning, business writing, web site design, marketing, fund-raising, and team-building. The speaker listed corporations who value volunteer service, and job candidates who have coupled classroom studies with applied experience. The speaker used a topical organization to divide the body of her speech into three areas, finding a volunteer placement offering marketable skills, creating a portfolio to document competencies, and jobs available in the public sector.

Students performing community service for a public speaking course typically choose the experience as a speech topic. Required to keep a service journal, students draw upon recorded impressions to craft compelling presentations with a human face. Gleaned from several of my courses, the results of such efforts follow. This chapter presents student speeches that employed the tools of informative speaking and left a lasting impact on classmates and this instructor. The results of their efforts may also encourage you to pursue the challenges and rewards of service-learning and to see the natural application of communication concepts to public service. Analyses and exercises are provided to help you develop an informative service-learning speech with a clear objective, effective organization, a compelling introduction and conclusion, and strong visual complement.

DEFINING THE OBJECTIVES OF INFORMATIVE SERVICE-LEARNING DISCOURSE

Because community service may arouse deep feelings about social needs, a speaker's ambition to communicate the full scope of an issue may conflict with the need to limit a topic to an achievable objective. Despite the temptation to do so, no one can correct a deeply seated social problem with a single speech. Productively tackling illiteracy is better served by profiling the specific mission of a local reading program rather than describing the endemic problem. To manage the scope of a speech, a speaker should first express a specific objective in a single sentence, precisely stating the desired audience response (e.g., "I want my audience to understand the prerequisites for serving as an America Reads mentor."). Here are the steps to guide a student from an unmanageable global issue to an achievable subject for a 5 to 7 minute speech:

1. Write a sentence stating the reaction you seek from listeners. The objective, "I want my audience to appreciate the causes and effects of homelessness," deserves an entire book. Ask yourself, "what is the most important thing about homelessness I want my listeners to understand?"

44

2. Refine your general first statement to express a more specific and concrete audience reaction (e.g., "My audience should understand the four most common causes of homelessness."). The speaker has pared the subject to causes, rather than both cause and effect, and limits the focus to principle causes. Yet, the still general subject is unlikely to generate interest in any specific service agency attempting to ameliorate the causes of homelessness.

3. Rewrite the statement until it expresses a specific and tangible audience response. The speaker finally expresses a clear and concrete objective stating, "I want my listeners to understand how the group Swords to Plowshares provides rehabilitation counseling and jobs for veterans." Such topic refinement produces a specifically targeted presentation more likely to motivate prospective volunteers or donors. A less directed subject often generates enthusiasm that quickly evaporates.

AUDIENCE ANALYSIS

Audience analysis is vital to the service-learning presentation. By soliciting class opinion, a student found that many in her public speaking class considered community service as glorified "go-fer" work that had little impact on social problems. Recognizing this predisposition, she composed a speech entitled, "Will Your Volunteer Service Help Cure Cancer?" Opening her speech with this inflated title produced intended laughter, but also addressed the widespread skepticism her audience held about the value of community service. Acknowledging opposing attitudes addresses the principle of inoculation theory (see Chapter 6). Accordingly, she devised a realistic strategy to overcome objections. Her opening statement follows.

> *"Will your volunteer service help cure cancer? The short answer is no, but as Gandhi replied to a disciple who questioned the meager contribution of his service to strife-torn India, 'But your deeds will mean much to you.'"*

Her speech described the sense of personal accomplishment derived from "improving the quality of your own universe." She recounted her experience with a literacy program, stating,

Did I eradicate illiteracy in America? No, but imagine my reaction to a 5th grader who read at a 2nd grade level before our tutoring sessions, calling me with the news, 'I just finished my first big book!' His excitement moved mountains for me. The America Reads branch on campus offers training for mentors who wish to make a personal contribution to fighting illiteracy.

This concrete example encouraged some skeptical listeners to see themselves as volunteers producing tangible results.

Contrary to the skeptical audience, some groups are ready adherents to community service. A student also addressing the America Reads program, but speaking before an audience of education majors, titled her speech, "Join the War against Illiteracy." The daunting goal of eradicating illiteracy appealed to prospective teachers. They identified with the speaker's metaphor of "joining the army in the battle against illiteracy." While audiences skeptical of large-scale service programs may resist this broad-brush approach, future teachers committed to teaching thousands of children over a long career saw the ambitious endeavor as heroic.

You may better understand your classmates' views of key social issues than their commitment to community service. In a course offering service-learning, take note of preliminary reactions to your instructor's introduction of this unit. You may informally quiz a cross-section of classmates, or more formally devise a questionnaire to determine their attitudes toward community service.

Class Activity

Almost every community has an historical society dedicated to protecting architectural landmarks. Typically, the membership of such organizations consists of older citizens who possess more leisure time and closer attachment to community history. Groups dedicated to historical preservation have succeeded in saving architecturally significant buildings from demolition and passing zoning ordinances to maintain the harmony and aesthetic value of historical districts.

In a time of rapid economic change, historical landmarks are often considered commercially outmoded and unprofitable. Under such conditions, saving such icons requires full community commitment. Involving a young audience in the mission of a local historical society requires a creatively tailored informative presentation. Download the web site of a local historical society. In problem-solving groups, determine how the information on the site could be incorporated into an informational speech that would interest a college audience in the goals of the organization.

ORGANIZING INFORMATION TO STRENGTHEN THE MESSAGE

Audiences better comprehend well-organized presentations. As discussed in Chapter 6, selection of the best means for organizing your service-learning presentation is critical to your success. After first determining your objective, consider what organizational pattern best conveys your ideas. Sketching trial outlines with different patterns is an excellent means for determining the varied impact of each design, and which best suits your purpose.

After assessing the utility of several organizational patterns, a student volunteering for the Exploratorium, an interactive science museum in San Francisco, found that elementary school audiences responded best to a speech using a compare/contrast design. His rationale follows:

> *Children raised in the computer age respond well to hands-on learning. Popular electronic educational games allow young players to participate in the act of learning. Unlike the staid art gallery, requiring hushed voices and prohibiting touch, Exploratorium visitors discover scientific principles by waving electronic wands, mixing exotic solutions, and striking melodious pipes. Shouts of awe and discovery are welcomed. A speech design comparing and contrasting behavioral ground rules at the Exploratorium with those of the fine arts museum makes the idea of science education exciting.*

A student wishing to inform listeners of services offered by local homeless shelters first weighed interpretations of a chronological model. For one option, she considered tracing the steady increase of homelessness over the last three decades, and the community's attempt to meet the growing numbers. She quickly discarded as misguided her second option, a vast chronology of homelessness starting with the role of medieval cathedrals as sanctuaries for the poor. A third time-based interpretation developed the progressive mental and physical deterioration of homeless individuals who refuse professional care. Reminding herself of her goal to describe the resources and volunteer opportunities of local shelters, she selected a topical design that sequentially described the counseling, nutritional, and health services provided by local shelters. In post speech remarks she confessed,

"At first I got carried away by trying to cover too much. For a moment, I even considered force-fitting my love for European history into my speech. Assessing the merits of each organizational model brought me back to my real goal."

Choosing the method of organization that best meets your objectives has enormous impact on the development and success of your message. Experiment with different designs to determine which suits your goal.

Class Activity

Your campus probably has a support program for students with disabilities. Such programs typically include a professional staff and a legion of student volunteers. Volunteers perform such services as note-taking for those with limited motor skills, reading to the visually impaired, and comprehension work for those with information retention difficulties. Visit the disabilities center on campus and obtain information about the services and volunteer opportunities the center provides. In small groups, first establish the objective of an informative speech focused on the disabilities center. Next, briefly discuss how different organizational patterns would influence the development of the speech. Choose the pattern that best meets your chosen objective and sketch an outline using that method of organization. Share your ideas with the class.

WRITING COMPELLING INTRODUCTIONS AND CONCLUSIONS

After you have determined your objective and have chosen an organizational pattern, you need an introduction that gains the attention of your listeners and showcases the promise of your subject. You no doubt can recall hearing blanket introductions that squandered the opportunity to generate interest. "Today I'm going to describe the rewards of serving as a Big Brother or a Big Sister," qualifies as an example. How much more engaging to open with a story of a Big Brother or Sister taking a wide-eyed seven year old to a first baseball game or natural history museum. Let the compelling story create initial interest with the theme of volunteering for this mentoring organization.

The need to first engage your audience is critical to the service-learning presentation, as listeners may have little knowledge of your subject. This section includes sample introductions illustrating a variety of techniques to create interest and establish purpose for a service-learning speech. You will then write your own introduction to meet the challenge of a realistic and challenging case study.

To encourage my students to compare the advantages of different types of introductions, I devise an activity providing background information on an educational program devoted to interdisciplinary curriculum development. Students devise different introductions to determine which best generates interest in the benefits and volunteer opportunities of the program. An activity using a single subject highlights the qualities of different types of introductions. The following section presents a variety of approaches to introduce the For Spacious Skies program, a cross-disciplinary K-12 curriculum used nationally by thousands of teachers.

Narrative

Even in our age of multimedia stimulation, audiences are still riveted by an intriguing story. The compelling story generates characters and situations arousing curiosity, empathy, personal connection, and humor. As a result, we want to know the story's outcome, its moral, or its message. The well-conceived story presents the critically important human element of community service.

One student approached the exercise with this story describing the genesis of the For Spacious Skies program.

> *Boston weatherman Jack Borden awoke refreshed from a nap under the autumnal sky that stretched over the Appalachian Mountains. Away from urban congestion, noise, and pollution, he lay in his sleeping bag transfixed by the beauty of the sky. The deep blue sky, filled with golden edged clouds, looked like a giant canvas of glorious natural art. He had an epiphany. His surest instincts told him that the sky could serve as a learning instrument if we simply learned to see it as a constantly changing artifact. This morning I will share how Jack Borden's realization led to the For Spacious Skies program, an integrated approach to learning that has boosted the reading level, aesthetic awareness, writing skills, and scientific literacy of thousands of students across the country.*

Startling Statement

A startling statement quickly grabs the attention of listeners. The following example demonstrates how a speaker used this provocative technique to create interest in the potential of the For Spacious Skies program.

What if I told you that there is a resource for elementary schools that boosts reading comprehension, writing and critical thinking skills by 15 to 20%? Then what if I told you that this program is free and available to everyone? As future teachers or parents, you would want to learn more about this unique, creative, and cost-free resource, the For Spacious Skies program. This evening I will describe how this program promotes a hands-on, integrated curriculum that increases academic performance and changes forever the way children look at their everyday world. You will also learn how you can become involved in promoting this program in your school district.

Personal Reference

All introductions must engage listeners. But an introduction that includes the audience as participants reaches a unique level of involvement. Using his training as a filmmaker, a student designed an introduction inspired by the principle of the first-person camera to achieve audience participation. Cinematically, this technique records action from the audience's vantage rather than from the view of a character or neutral perspective. An audience member's eyes become virtual camera lenses. The following introduction uses this technique to heighten listener involvement.

You open your bedroom window, awakened by a searing noise and a brilliant light. Standing in your darkened bedroom, you gaze upon a luminous moon, ten times its usual brightness. Raise your finger and trace the racing path of a star leaving golden waves in its wake. Have you awakened from a dream? No, you behold the surreal scene of Vincent van Gogh's "Starry Night." Teachers across the nation use such marvelous sky images to inspire creative writing, science and history lessons, and much more. I will tell you how the For Spacious Skies curriculum has put passion back into learning.

Deferred Thesis

An ambitious teacher, brimming with excitement about a dynamic new approach to teaching, led his 9th graders on a nighttime hike to a wooded lake. Teacher, students, and parents sat watching the sky turn pitch black, swallowing the view of the lake. The outing lasted until 10:30. Even the rain did not dampen the group's buoyant spirits. The students were doubly excited, out late on a school night and enjoying the rainy night under a canopy of pine. This intrepid group was there to experience the misty woods, the night sky, and to write poetry. "Even though there were no stars, the sky was present, and we could feel it moving within us," wrote the teacher. For his poem, one student wrote:

"It is dark
I am blinded by the absence of light
But I must think
No, I am not blind
I feel the sky with my hands
I can hear the sky with my ears
I can taste the sky with my mouth"

What produced this outpouring of excitement and creativity? This class was motivated by the For Spacious Skies program, a multidisciplinary K-12 curriculum that uses the sky and all that it inspires as its core. My presentation will describe how teachers across the country use this resource as the centerpiece for studying science, math, language arts, history, music and the arts. I will also describe how local teachers apply their own imagination to the program, and how you can get involved or learn more about this exciting curriculum.

Beginning this speech with a nighttime journey through the woods and withholding an early statement of purpose illustrates the introduction employing a deferred thesis. This technique typically presents an intriguing, humorous, poignant, or even mysterious story to arouse interest. Engaged in the story, listeners become eager to discover its purpose or outcome. Accordingly, the story must neatly dovetail into a concise statement of purpose and relevance, as does the above example.

Quotation

"As much as the most brilliant celestial jewel in the heavens, we are the stuff of stars. The cataclysmic birth of our universe sent forth energy and matter that formed the stars, the planets, and all of us."

This awe-inspiring quote by astronomer Carl Sagan was a physics major's opening statement for the For Spacious Skies exercise. A quote from a well-chosen source adds credibility and sometimes eloquence, emotion, testimony, conviction, or humor to an introduction. A direct quote is selected when it most meaningfully conveys a central idea. The Sagan quote was presented via videotape featuring the famous astronomer. The video's ethereal music, images of spectacular galaxies, and Sagan's persona, heightened the impact of the opening words. The 15 to 20-second video complemented, but did not dominate the presentation. This use of video illustrates how communication concepts overlap, in this case the use of an elegant, attention-getting quotation and a supportive visual aid. For the purpose of explanation, instructors typically describe concepts independently, but in practical use, communication concepts naturally combine. This effective use of videotape also paves the way for the next unit on using visual aids to underscore community issues.

An introduction creates the initial impression of your subject. Given the tendency of listeners to quickly determine their interest in a subject, I recommend that students write several introductions to determine the most effective way to capture audience interest. Of the various introductions to the For Spacious Skies program, discuss which was the most effective, and why?

Class Activity

Studies find that a majority of Americans lack basic first-aid skills and are unable to administer early, effective treatment for victims of heart attack, burns, shock, trauma, and other health emergencies. Assume that the Red Cross sponsors a first-aid course each semester for students and staff on your campus. In groups of five, each member should develop a different introduction to an informative speech describing the value of the campus first-aid program. From the five types of introductions presented earlier, each member should choose a different style. Each introduction should also fulfill the basic ingredients of a complete introduction (gain attention, and establish tone, purpose, audience relevance, and a bridge to the body of the speech).

Conclusions

Unlike persuasive discourse, the informative speech does not request attitudinal or behavioral change. Nonetheless, compelling information is often persuasive (e.g., the impact of statistics describing the correlation of smoking to lung cancer and cardiovascular disease).

Despite the importance of conclusions, speakers often invest little time in thoughtfully planning final remarks. Speeches that end abruptly, or with needless repetition, diminish the impact of the presentation. An effective conclusion should both reinforce main ideas and implant a memorable thought. Although there are a number of ways to conclude a speech, an elegant conclusion recaptures the tone and theme of the introduction. This artistic approach reconnects with the attention-getting opening, creating organizational symmetry. The following conclusion models this approach, recapturing the narrative-based introduction featuring For Spacious Skies founder Jack Borden.

> *Imagine a group of school children lying in a field of mountain daisies, looking skyward at a flotilla of white clouds. A girl is reminded of a Claude Monet painting that she saw in class. A boy thinks of an opening line for a sky poem he will write. Another classmate identifies the scientific term for the billowy clouds, cumulous.*
> *These children fulfill Jack Borden's inspired daydream of seeing the sky as an artifact containing the seeds for boundless learning. The Web site www.forspaciousskies.com describes how anyone can realize the potential of scanning the sky.*

Class Activity

Rejoin your group of five that completed the activity for writing introductions. With the introductions you each composed for the Red Cross first-aid exercise, design a conclusion using the symmetrical "bookend" principle of recapturing the theme and tone of your introduction.

AUDIO AND VISUAL AIDS

You have probably covered guidelines for designing effective audio and visual aids. Reviewing basic fundamentals, you know that visual aids should be clearly visible to the entire audience, communicate information clearly and concisely, and be displayed and removed at appropriate times. Beyond these basics, some speakers creatively design audio and visual aids vividly capturing the activities and benefits of volunteering. The following examples illustrate such resourcefulness.

In our television-dominated culture, video is an attractive complement to public speech. Nevertheless, videotape carries potential for abuse. A speaker may show three minutes of poorly edited video for a five-minute speech. The ragged video compromises the credibility of the speaker and the impact of the message. Visual aids should serve, not drive the message.

Videotape powerfully reinforces the message when used appropriately. A volunteer for the Special Olympics used a 30 second video clip to record the girl's 60-yard dash, volunteers praising all runners at the finish, and the beaming winner framed by her proud parents. In 30 seconds the video captured the effort, spirit, and rewards of the games, graphic testimony to the value of the event.

Speakers often overlook the value of audiotape. One speaker played short segments from the Talking Book series to recreate her volunteer service with a visually impaired elderly gentleman. She opened her speech playing the first line of Dickens' David Copperfield.

"Whether I shall turn out to be the hero of my life, or whether that station will be held by anybody else, these pages must show."

She sat facing a chair draped with an old-fashioned quilt, symbolically representing her client. She recounted how her love for literature drew her to the assisted reading program. The simulated environment recreated her afternoons of playing literature to a man who could no longer read his beloved classics.

Her conclusion contained the opening of a Tale of Two Cities, interpreted by a superb dramatic reader.

It was the best of times, it was the worst of times, it was the age of wisdom, it was the age of foolishness, it was the epoch of belief, it was the epoch of incredulity, it was the season of Light, it was the season of Darkness, it was the spring of hope, it was the winter of despair...

She described how Dickens' words *"brought a satisfied smile to my devoted listener, he devouring the words as if they were tasty morsels of a gourmet meal."* Besides demonstrating the rewards of these sessions, the well-chosen nineteenth century passages addressed universal themes relevant to a contemporary audience, questioning the realization of our heroic self-images, and recognizing cultural contradictions still present. The audio selections and props recreated her experience for the audience, vividly portraying the human element of service-learning.

I encourage linking fine arts images with service presentations and providing examples illustrating how visual icons dynamically reinforce a central message. For his opening remarks, a speaker displayed a famous photograph of John Muir standing beside Yosemite Falls.

Naturalist John Muir founded the Sierra Club to preserve the American wilderness for future generations. He posed by these

> *magnificent falls to symbolically support naming Yosemite Valley a national park. Photographs of this Sierra jewel finally convinced Congress to grant National Park status.*
>
> *But National Park status has not completely safeguarded Yosemite. The Disney Corporation nearly succeeded in installing a chair lift alongside the fall, treating the site like a theme park. The Sierra Club is dedicated to preserving wilderness, allowing your grandchildren to stand in the footsteps of John Muir. The organization depends on an army of volunteers to promote Muir's vision. I will describe the variety of ways volunteers may serve this noble cause.*

The famous Muir photograph fits the resonance theory model (see Chapter 6) of incorporating information consonant with audience experience. Numerous parks, streets, schools, and foundations in the university's locale carry Muir's name. The image presents an esteemed historical figure and supports the flow of the introduction. This integration of language and photograph creates the ingredients for lasting imagery.

Realizing the benefits of fine arts and service-learning discourse, one speaker used a Picasso street scene to dramatically depict homelessness. The painter's Blue Period uses somber colors to heighten the emotional impact of isolation and despair. Another speaker chose Pulitzer Prize winning photographs chronicling human rights violations to encourage support of Amnesty International. The applied nature of service-learning helps to deliver art from the rarefied museum to the service of everyday human needs.

Also in the realm of still imagery, consider bringing your camera to your volunteer assignment. Photographs of your service enhance your credibility by documenting your experience and underscoring the meaningfulness of your service. A student describing the volunteer opportunities of a summer sports program displayed slides of himself demonstrating a tennis stroke to a circle of inner-city children. A slide of a broadly smiling 12 year-old girl hoisting a winner's trophy added enormous impact to his conclusion.

> *"Shawna may not become the next Serena Williams, but she beams with new confidence, having excelled in a sport once considered the domain of the country club set."*

Well-chosen photographs also enhance the organization of an informative speech, as evidenced by a student who supported a compare/contrast design with before and after slides of a community planting drive to restore the barren dunes of an abused shoreline. The resourceful selection of visual aids depicts the human element of community service. Creatively think of visual aids that transport listeners to the frontlines of service, leaving them with lasting images of the value of volunteering.

Class Activity:

A food bank can help you organize a campus food drive. The bank provides everything needed to collect cans of food and booklets describing how to design posters and flyers. The food bank collects all donations at the conclusion of the drive. These drives are essential for maintaining the stocks of food banks, supplying more than 20% of inventories. This 20% is critical because it helps add key food stuffs for balanced nutrition. Says one food bank director, *"Manufacturers typically donate things like 100,000 boxes of cereal or 300 cherry pies. People can't live on just cereal and pie. Without food drives, we couldn't provide well-rounded meals."*

Your group is assigned to develop a two to three-minute speech with visual aids that volunteer speakers will present before a variety of classes informing students of the food drive and recommended donations. Design a message incorporating visual aids complementing both rational and dramatic elements of your text. Rational data may include the percentage of food bank donations supplied by drives, the number of needy served, food deposit locations, etc. Dramatic information typically involves human-interest narratives. Annotate your text with a variety of ideas for visual support. Like the preceding examples, take a creative approach to your selection of visual aids. Share your ideas with the class.

References

Bok, B. (1996). *Social Responsibility of the Modern University*. Cambridge, Mass: Harvard University Press.

Coles, Robert. (1993). *The Call to Service*. New York: Houghton Mifflin.

Collier, J & Collier, M. (1986). *Visual Anthropology: Photography as a Research Method*. Albuquerque, NM: University of New Mexico Press.

Jaffe, C. (1995). *Public Speaking: A Cultural Perspective*. Belmont, CA:
Wadsworth/Thomson Learning.

Leff, M. (1983). Topical Invention and Metaphoric Interaction. *The
Southern Speech Communication Journal*, 48, 214-229.

Verderber, R. (2000). *The Challenge of Effective Speaking*. Belmont, CA:
Wadsworth/Thomson Learning.

Wilder, Lilyan (1986). *Professionally Speaking*: New York: Simon and
Schuster, Inc.

CHAPTER 5

DESIGNING EFFECTIVE PERSUASIVE SERVICE-LEARNING PRESENTATIONS

THE ROLE OF THEORIES AND METHODS OF PERSUASION

Perhaps the noblest application of persuasive communication is on behalf of community service. Community programs we take for granted could not have been established without the compelling use of persuasion to convince legislators and mobilize voters and volunteers. Public service announcements urge us to assign designated drivers, recognize the dangers of drugs, practice safe sex, or obtain an annual breast or prostate examination. These messages are designed and delivered by professionals with considerable experience in applied persuasion.

Research finds that the effort of developing and delivering a persuasive message in support of community service reinforces one's commitment to the stated cause. But beyond this intra-personal effect, designing an effective persuasive service-learning presentation requires the selection of theories and strategies that blend community need with the interests and values of an audience.

While your class explores theories and techniques of persuasion, this chapter offers examples of how such concepts can translate to effective advocacy for community service. You will find discussions of student presentations that apply theories of persuasion, methods of organization, selection of evidence, audience analysis, appropriate emotional tone, evocative language, visual aids, and nonverbal communication. This chapter also presents examples of alternative media forums, such as a low-cost guerrilla media campaign that alerted an entire campus to a personal safety issue. Problem-solving exercises are included to further enhance your skill as an advocate for community service.

RESONANCE THEORY

This author subscribes to Tony Schwartz's view that persuasion is best achieved through the combined efforts of source and receiver. This concept maintains that an audience's experiences are as important to attitude change as the speaker's message. The theory maintains that experiences are not stored as abstract symbols, but as recollections of real-life and tangible feelings. Tapping into these feelings is best accomplished with a dramatic message that evokes a personal experience (e.g., a commercial for a car battery depicting a stranded motorist, something most drivers have experienced). Projecting feelings and experiences the sender shares with the audience strikes a resonant chord and facilitates persuasion.

This chapter utilizes extracts of speeches by former students enrolled in this author's persuasive speaking course. The included student presentation employed resonance theory as a strategy to address the case study entitled, "Promoting Literacy through Storytelling." The following section includes the case problem, an extract of a solution presented in the student speech, an analysis of the speech, and an exercise encouraging you to apply your own persuasive strategies to the problem.

Promoting Literacy through Storytelling
The public libraries in a diverse urban community offer an after-school and Saturday morning storytelling session. The program requires numerous volunteer readers, as each session offers three levels of storytelling (for ages 4-7, 8-11, and 12-14). The program is designed to stimulate interest in reading, library use, and discussion of literature.

Over the last several years attendance at the sessions has fallen by 50%. Says one librarian, "I fear that this trend will continue, given the appeal of electronic media that so captivate today's children."

Too many children now read poorly and find the mall arcade more appealing than the library. Given a general disinterest in reading, and the difficulty of recruiting engaging readers, the library's storytelling program may cease to exist.

Objective
Your task is to develop a 2 to 3 minute presentation promoting the library's storytelling program. You may direct your speech to a group of parents, teachers, or an elementary or middle school classroom. Highlight or

underline sections of your presentation that illustrate use of a theory or technique of persuasion learned in class. In a preface to your outline, identify your audience, the setting, and your specific purpose. In a post outline remark, name and define the employed theory and state your reasoning for its selection.

Extract of Student Speech Employing Resonance Theory:
- *Audience: Fifth grade elementary school class*
- *Purpose: To use Schwartz's Resonance Theory to motivate the young audience to attend a storytelling featuring <u>The Lord of the Rings</u> by J.R.R. Tolkien.*

I bet that most of you recognize my tall, pointed wizard's hat and the lightning bolt birthmark on my forehead as belonging to a famous character in a magical story. ("Harry Potter" the speaker's audience chimed in unison). How many of you have read at least the first book in the J.K. Rowling series, Harry Potter and the Sorcerer's Stone, describing Harry's first experiences at the Hogwarts' School for Wizards? (Many in the fifth grade audience raise their hand).
I have heard from a number of children your age that the first Harry Potter book got them excited about reading. That was the case for my nephew, also a fifth grader. But while he is counting the days until the next Harry Potter book goes on sale, he never wants the series to end. The world of Harry Potter is just too wonderful to leave. I am here to tell you that it never has to end. The Harry Potter books that you treasure can lead to other amazing worlds of wizards and folk, both magical and menacing. In fact, my hat is not a replica of Harry Potter's. It belongs to Gandalf, the most famous wizard in all literature. Gandalf lived in Middle Earth, in a time and place, if you will excuse, long, long ago and far, far away. Middle Earth is the setting for <u>Lord of the Rings</u> by J.R.R. Tolkien. This trilogy will introduce you to an even larger world of wizards, elves, dwarfs, hobbits, slimy goblins, and orcs.
The Lord of the Rings is the evil Sauron, who forged a series of gold rings, one of which bestows unequaled power to its possessor. Quite by accident, the ring falls into the hands of a humble hobbit. The ring holds spell over all who depend on its powers. Gandalf tells the hobbit, Frodo, of the dangers of owning the ring and of Lord Sauron's relentless search for it. Frodo embarks on a dangerous quest through places both enchanted and terrifying to cast the ring

into the fires where it was forged, destroying its power forever. If Harry Potter wetted your taste for Wizardry, magic, and adventure, visit your public library for the scheduled readings of Lord of the Rings and enter a wondrous world you will never forget.

Student's Rationale for Using Resonance Theory

My introduction uses resonance theory to exploit the common experiences and the emotional attachment many kids have with Harry Potter. Even kids in my audience who had not read the books know about them and understand their popularity. Although literary critics view Lord of the Rings as more sophisticated than the Potter books, it is part of the same fantasy genre. Evoking the excitement, anticipation, and captivating fantasy of Harry Potter books and associating these emotions and memories with Lord of the Rings, uses the principle of sympathetic resonance.

Class Activity

In small groups devise an alternative means for using resonance theory to promote the city library's storytelling program. Craft a 2 to 3 minute presentation (it may be in full-sentence outline form), underlining or highlighting the section of the text that reflects the use of resonance theory. In post outline remarks, state your reasoning for your specific application of the theory.

INOCULATION THEORY

Inoculation theory is one of the most intriguing concepts of persuasive communication, as it centers on preventing susceptibility to persuasion. The term derives from the medical immunization model. A flu shot exposes us to a small dose of a virus, too little to generate the illness, but enough to activate the body's resistance to it. Inoculation in persuasion exposes receivers to selective and weakened doses of a counter argument, followed by a refutation of that argument. A preemptive presentation and refutation of argument "A" will diminish the impact of subsequent exposure to a proponent arguing for "A."

Inoculation techniques are often used early in a persuasive message, helping to prevent audiences from internalizing counter arguments to the speaker's position. Examine how a student used the inoculation principle to promote volunteering in a senior convalescent center. (Note underlined section).

We live in an age when our elderly are often removed from family life to spend their remaining time in a convalescent center. In past generations the extended family cared for its elders. With families now often dispersed and needing two-incomes, this traditional care-giving model has crumbled. Yet, the need of the elderly for close human contact is unchanged. Volunteering in a convalescent center can help fill this basic human need.

Because we live apart from our elderly and in a culture obsessed with preserving youth, our society has developed an avoidance reaction to old age. Many of college age have never visited a convalescent center or have felt uncomfortable in that environment. You may view volunteering in that setting as depressing, or that you have no meaningful skills to offer. Some of you have read news stories critical of the quality of care in convalescent centers and wish no part of them. A friend who visited her grandmother, an Alzheimer's patient, found that she did not recognize her own granddaughter. 'I'm not going back. I'd rather remember her the way she was,' said my friend. Haven't some of you made similar rationalizations?

My friend's remarks hit home. I also have a grandparent with Alzheimer's and had all of the above reasons for rarely visiting him. Then I heard about a program that changed me from a grandchild with an avoidance problem to a weekly volunteer, reconnected with his grandfather, and with many of the patients at his convalescent home. Through the Share a Pet Program, sponsored by the S.P.C.A., I bring Charlie, my loving Labrador Retriever to the center most Saturday mornings. Charlie's welcoming, if wet demonstrations of love, have initiated my conversations with patients who once sat expressionless when I passed by. I have seen smiles and heard sweet talk come from bedridden patients after receiving dog licks of unconditional love. Spending more time at the center, I have met other volunteers who have found their niche. Some enjoy reading literature to patients who cannot track words on a page. Even my sister's mediocre piano playing is eagerly anticipated by large groups of patients. I have learned that the dog, the book, and the instrument are media for human connection. Within each of you is the means to make similar connections that can help relieve the estrangement of our once revered elderly. Today I am going to tell you how you can find your niche and begin to repay the debt that we all owe to those who preceded us.

Class Activity

The Inoculation model serves as an excellent tool for overcoming audience doubts about community service. In a typical college class many may have no volunteer experience. Some carry full academic loads and part-time jobs and may question stretching an already over-committed schedule. Others may see volunteer work as meaningless "go-fer" work. The prospect of serving in a "bad neighborhood" or with an unfamiliar population may intimidate others. Some may question if a placement could meet their interests or boost employment credentials. Individually, or in small groups, develop an introduction to a speech that incorporates inoculation theory as a means to overcome some of the above objections.

CREDIBILITY

You have probably studied the importance of establishing credibility to the success of a message or a movement. When appointed to head Kids at Risk, former Joint Chief of Staff and Secretary of State Colin Powell, brought instant stature to this national effort to help youth overcome problems like illiteracy, drug abuse, violence and unemployment. Would Time and Newsweek magazines have devoted cover stories to this movement if a capable, but unknown person had been selected as its leader?

Credibility depends upon a message recipient's perception of the believability, trustworthiness, and status of a communicator or organization. As you perform volunteer service, your perceived credibility will influence your success.

Credibility is multi-faceted. One study found that volunteers soliciting donations received more contributions when wearing official looking uniforms. Appropriate dress is part of the credibility package. A student volunteer sometimes dressed as the classic fairytale author, Hans Christian Andersen, when telling stories to elementary school children. He reported that his young audiences seemed more transported to the realm of fantasy when he donned the period costume. He also told his audience that he chose this volunteer activity because he loved to write stories for his siblings and had published two in a children's magazine. These activities did not make him the next Maurice Sendak, but they buttressed the perception of his sincerity and professionalism, ingredients adding layers to his credibility with his young audience.

Class Activity

You, or your group, have volunteered to serve as docents for a local museum. You may determine the type of museum (e.g., classic fine art, ethnic art, music, vintage automobile, Native American, sports). Your duties call for you or your group members to lead tours of the museum. Museum patrons understand that you are a volunteer, but desire expertise and a satisfying complement to their visit. Demonstrate how you would establish your credibility as a museum docent by doing the following:

1. Write the introduction you would deliver to tour members to build the expectation of a rewarding museum visit.
2. Provide two brief extracts from your presentation that support your knowledge of the subject.
3. What interactive elements with tour members could you design to enrich the quality of the tour?
4. What attire would best suit your role and authority?
5. Describe other factors that would add to your credibility as museum docent.

EMOTIONAL APPEALS

Everyone has seen a highly charged televised public service spot such as the image of a frying egg with the voiceover, "This is your brain on drugs." Even rational appeals, like statistics describing the health risks of smoking, may elicit fear. Teens may feel especially threatened by messages about the social consequences of dandruff or acne.

Provoking fear often proves an irresistible device for those communicating the urgency of a community need. But before implementing this tempting tool, the relative success of fear appeals should be assessed. In surveying the vast research on the effects of low, moderate, or high levels of threat in persuasive communication, current studies conclude that high fear arousal produces optimal attitude change when satisfying certain conditions. High fear arousal is most effective if receivers perceive themselves as vulnerable, accept the effectiveness of proposed solutions to the threat, and view the message source as highly credible. Studies have revealed that low or moderate levels of fear are often more effective absent these elements.

The use of fear arousal poses intriguing consequences for the service-learning speech. Suppose that you wish to promote volunteer service for a literacy project to a well-educated middle-class college audience that has not experienced the stigma of illiteracy. How would you encourage your listeners to perceive themselves as vulnerable? Here is the opening of a student speech that tackled this problem.

> *Does it shock you to hear that 25% of our nation's high school graduates are functionally illiterate? This statistic does not account for a national 20% high school dropout rate that includes a functional illiteracy rate of over 50%. A report issued by the America Reads Project, a national program that links thousands of university educators and volunteers, describes the ripple effect of illiteracy, 'as removing the stepping stones to learning, and self-development.'*
>
> *In our modern service economy knowledge is our most important resource, but the United States rates 16th in the world in academic achievement. Is it any wonder that tiny Finland is a giant in the mobile phone industry? Why do you think that our high technology companies lobby to increase the immigration quotas for skilled foreign workers to fill the thousands of vacant high-paying jobs?*
>
> *Although this audience is highly educated, we will all share the consequences of economic decline, higher unemployment and crime rates, unless we address our scandalous illiteracy problem. We will all contribute to this social emergency unless we become involved in the solution. You can play a significant role in revitalizing our literacy standards by committing five hours a week to America Reads, an organization committed to having every student read at or above grade level. Today I will tell you how you can become a trained America Reads tutor, and be given the resources to make an impact in your community.*

The level of fear arousal in this introduction is perhaps low to moderate. More hard-hitting specifics about economic and social consequences affecting the immediate audience could have moved this message into the moderate to high fear registers. Nonetheless, the speaker adroitly expanded the scope of the threat to include listeners, provided a means for acting on threat reduction, and bolstered credibility by citing statistics issued by a respected national organization. All three steps theoretically enhance the efficacy of fear arousal in persuasive communication.

Class Activity

In a small group, imagine that you are a team of interns assigned to draft a one-minute public service announcement for your campus radio station on an issue that potentially provokes student fear (security, building contamination, health, etc.). First discuss the value of using a level of fear arousal in your radio text. When might this tactic be effective or ineffective? Remember that fear appeals do not exclude the use of rational or testimonial evidence. Before crafting the final message, establish a rationale for your strategy based on what you know about principles of persuasion.

IMAGERY

Language can paint pictures or speakers can find compelling visual aids to add impact to presentations. Whether building imagery through language or presenting a visual aid, speakers should search for words that convey emotion, scale, and texture. Evocative language heightens appreciation and understanding of a subject. A plea for community involvement may present rates of homelessness and child abuse and still not move many to action. Rational data often requires the complement of a narrative with a human face to carry full impact. As the volunteer coordinator for the San Francisco Park District said,

> *I gave dozens of speeches detailing the tons of garbage left by weekend park visitors. But I started seeing an increase in volunteer litter collectors when I told a story about the bonding experience of a family who worked as a team on Sunday afternoons picking up garbage. I described in detail the specific pockets of the park they considered their personal garden. The images of family and their proclaimed special garden gave audiences an emotional and tangible picture of the rewards of service.*

An urban development director lobbying for more low-cost housing, maintained that legislators were moved by images of a single mother who used his program to move her children from the crime-ridden projects into a quiet home with a garden. The program required that she and her family assist with painting and finishing off the house. "This real scenario of benefit coupled with commitment motivated fence-sitting representatives to support expansion of the program."

A recruiter for a program sponsoring wilderness trips for inner-city children also relies on imagery to capture the experience for young campers.

Living in an environment continuously flooded by artificial light, these kids had never seen the gauzy veil of the Milky Way stretched across pitch-black canvas of night sky. Tightly clustered around quiet campfire light, these kids, so filled with frenetic energy that first day, sat still and reflective, in awe of the kaleidoscopic star show. But the pyrotechnics were yet to begin. While tracking satellites moving across the darkened stage like starry messengers, the first luminous cascade of crystal blue streaked across the sky. Long into the night, past any reasonable bedtime, a chorus of 'wows' and 'incredible' followed the fountains, cascades, and bending waves of shimmering light. These kids had seen the Aurora Borealis, the Northern Lights. They returned to their world changed.

Class Activity

As you promote community service, determine how imagery can add dimension and impact to your presentation. Discuss social issues or problems that are typically described quantitatively (e.g., unemployment, global warming, and pollution). What image-building words and narratives could you use to add human interest or tangible meaning to the data associated with one such issue?

BURKE'S PENTAD

Just as Monroe's Motivated Sequence has become a classic model for organizing a persuasive speech, Kenneth Burke's Pentad remains a time-honored model for holistically deconstructing the ingredients of a persuasive event. But while the pentad has been chiefly used as an analytic device, it also serves as a thorough blueprint for systematically planning the architecture of a persuasive strategy.

Let's define the parts of the pentad and illustrate how each was represented in a speech delivered by President Clinton in Utah when he dedicated a parcel of federal land as protected wilderness.

1. **Scene:** The place where the action/event occurs.
   Clinton did not issue his proclamation from distant Washington D.C., but from the Utah site. He delivered his speech framed by two magnificent sandstone pillars. This scene reinforces the magnificence of the public lands and the wisdom of protecting it.

2. **Act:** The action taking place.
   Clinton's speech proclaiming the protected status of the territory constituted the act. Key congressional supporters and environmental activists flanked the President while he spoke. The President's appearance strengthened his political alliance with these groups. Clinton, a public speaking virtuoso, also chose a medium that showcases his leadership talents.

3. **Agent:** The person(s) engaged in the act.
   The Secretary of the Interior often makes such dedications. But Presidents sometimes take such opportunities to cultivate a political image.

4. **Agency:** The means of delivering the message.
   Even though the event was a regional public speech, national television was the target medium. Utah residents were divided over the land reclassification, as some believed that commercial revenues would be lost. But television was the ideal medium to reach a national audience that generally favors expansion of wilderness lands.

5. **Purpose:** The objective of the event.
   Besides any altruistic motivation, the event, carried by all major national news services, portrayed Clinton as a guardian of our natural heritage and as an activist President.

Sophisticated applications of Burke's model manipulate interactions of pentad elements, like choosing an agency that best suits a particular agent. In the 1960's Marshall McLuhan developed a parallel idea, contending that the immediate character of television had altered mainstream communication, creating a taste for greater informality. He noted that television stars of the 1950's were often known by their first or familiar names, like Lucy or Uncle Milton. Today, we easily recognize Oprah, Regis, and Ellen. The intimate character of television often creates the perception that formal communicators are wooden. Al Gore's tendency for dry, over-articulation becomes the source of jokes on late night television. The more relaxed, conversational style of Bill Clinton exemplifies an increasing preference for what Kathleen Hall Jamieson calls the interpersonal voice.

In an address to a young audience during the Kids at Risk convocation, Colin Powell eschewed his usual conservative suit and tie for an open collar shirt and jeans. His speech contained an abundance of collective personal pronouns. Employing a self-disclosing interpersonal style, he recounted his early experiences with racism, and how the intervention of adult mentors prevented a wrong turn. Powell's style sent the message that it's time to shuck formal pieties, roll up our sleeves and meet the street-level problems of life. This approach reflects the more direct, immediate style that McLuhan predicted would result from the changing character of media. Burkian theory would call this a strategic blending of agent and agency.

Class Activity

You are the communication director for a non-profit group advocating increased funding for music and arts programs in K-12 public schools. You are assigned to orchestrate a public service announcement arguing that music and the arts are essential to a rounded education. Considering each element of Burke's Pentad, what recommendations would you make for the following? Explain your reasoning for each step.

1. **Scene:**   Describe the background or environment you would choose for the message sender.
2. **Act:**   What kind of communication would the source deliver?
3. **Agent:**   What kind of person best suits the purpose of the message?
4. **Agency:**   What medium/media would carry the message?
5. **Purpose:**   The agent could propose a variety of actions. Given the confines of time (a 60 second spot) and the dangers of an overly ambitious request, what specific proposals would your agent make?

ANALYZING AUDIENCE NEEDS

Successful persuasion starts with an analysis of audience makeup and needs. For community service presentations, the assessment of needs for different audiences is especially important. You may have already studied Maslow's theory of needs and his model that contends people generally require the fulfillment of basic life-sustaining needs before they are motivated by the higher needs for esteem and self-actualization. Persuading middle-class college students to volunteer for an elementary school breakfast program requires a different strategy than one trying to convince eligible parents to enroll their children in the program. The college audience, probably less preoccupied with everyday sustenance, would best respond to incentives aimed at the higher strata of Maslow's needs hierarchy, the need to pursue enhancement of self. Potential program recipients may respond better to the incentive that a good breakfast is the most sustaining meal of the day, as evidenced by improvement in the students' alertness, demeanor and achievement in school.

Class Activity

A local AIDS foundation trains volunteers to serve as phone operators for a hotline. Volunteers frequently answer sensitive questions, offer referrals, and provide emotional support. Aside from asking questions about HIV, callers often talk about relationships and other personal issues. The success of the hotline depends on motivating two populations, volunteers and callers (although a number of operators have contracted HIV and have lost friends and loved ones to the illness).

The foundation needs to develop different strategies for soliciting hotline volunteers and community appeals encouraging hotline use. How would you advise tailoring persuasive messages to address the different motivational needs of prospective volunteers and community members who would benefit from the services of the hotline?

Organizational Options

You may have already covered methods for organizing persuasive speeches. Speakers may choose from a variety of organizational patterns (e.g., problem-solution, chronological, spatial, topical, narrative, cause-effect) that can create a coherent message. But different organizational models may yield distinctively different topic interpretation and audience reaction. A persuader should select the pattern that best showcases key information and satisfies the goals of the speaker.

A student promoting Friends of the Urban Forest, a program dedicated to neighborhood tree planting, determined that a problem-solution design best fulfilled his objective, even though he had a talent for framing arguments chronologically. A chronological perspective could have described how modern development favors high-density construction over the more costly tree-lined streets of yesteryear. But the speaker's objective was to promote the multiple benefits of planting shade trees in poorer neighborhoods. Such trees could reduce the problems of costly summer air-conditioning and provide aesthetic value to homes' declining value. The speaker's goal clearly fit into a problem-solution framework.

Class Activity

The Meals on Wheels program provides delivery of hot meals to seniors unable to cook for themselves. Weekly groceries are supplied for those who can cook, but cannot shop for themselves. The personal contact for shut-in seniors with food providers is a vital part of the service. Food delivery volunteers are encouraged to get to know the background, needs and interests of the seniors they serve. Some volunteers deliver hot food or groceries daily, others once a week. In designing a speech to persuade classmates to volunteer for Meals on Wheels, discuss the benefits of using different methods of organization. Would one model better serve your recruitment objective? Or, would each organizational approach have its own merits?

RESOURCEFUL EVIDENCE

Using evidence effectively is fundamental to the development of persuasive arguments. As with any topic, an effective service-learning presentation offers a balanced array of evidence. A speech urging listeners to volunteer for the Special Olympics could present rational evidence (e.g., stating the number of participants), testimonial evidence (e.g., expert opinion citing the benefits to self-esteem for competitors) or narrative evidence (e.g., a compelling personal story of a competitor with cerebral palsy).

A type of support often underutilized is participation-based evidence. This involves the audience as a supportive workforce. We often see persuaders involve audiences, but usually in a rudimentary manner (e.g., "How many in the audience are certified in CPR?"). A former student employed a much more substantial and resourceful use of participation-based evidence in a speech calling for classmates to choose the service-learning option offered as a final project in my class. Having broad experience with a variety of community service agencies, she designed a volunteer survey distributed to classmates a week prior to her speech. The survey asked questions to determine the interests, skills, and social concerns of her audience. With the information gained from the survey, she sprinkled her speech with statements like,

Janice, I learned that you love gardening and think "that our lives would have less stress and more satisfaction if more people worked the soil and literally saw the fruits of their labor." Did you know that the famous chef Alice Waters developed a program instructing elementary schools how to create they own organic flower and vegetable garden? The kids grow fresh chemical-free vegetables and prepare their own salads and dishes from produce they have cultivated. Couldn't you see yourself spreading your own values and having fun by volunteering for this program?

The audience was both captivated and motivated by this degree of inclusion.

Directing arguments to audience character and needs is the cornerstone of persuasion. The resourceful use of participation-based evidence has the potential to jumpstart interest in community service. The creative use of such support should be far less rare.

DELIVERY AND NONVERBAL COMMUNICATION

When planning a persuasive speech, speakers often do not consider the impact of the nonverbal elements that can either help or hinder overall effectiveness. Culturally, we devote less conscious awareness to categorizing and assessing nonverbal than verbal meaning. Nonetheless, nonverbal factors significantly impact the persuasive process and should be carefully planned to serve the message.

Urging her audience to consider service as a hospice volunteer, a student carefully planned a nonverbal strategy to capture the institution's goal of helping terminal patients live their remaining time in the most comfortable and supportive environment possible.

Tailoring proxemic communication (the use of space), she discarded the formal speaker-audience separation of public distance. She sat in an open chair close to her audience; they seated in a tightly clustered semi-circle. She turned off the overhead lights and illuminated the classroom with softer candlelight. A technique used by storytellers, quiet candlelight heightens audience attention. Her loose-fitting white linen clothing further softened the atmosphere. She spoke in a soothing voice, easily heard despite its soft tone. During her speech she extended a hand in a comforting gesture to an imagined patient. Family and vacation photographs were placed on surrounding tables, as she stated, "spending one's last days with images of wonderful memories is a form of medicine that cannot be administered in a hospital."

A formal speech lacking thoughtful regard for the potential of nonverbal communication to establish mood, spirit, and even to even allay defensive reaction to the subject of death, would have missed the essence of volunteer hospice service.

Class Activity

Little League baseball in the inner-city is vanishing. Playgrounds with baseball fields are often empty. The reasons for this decline include the decay of facilities, the reputation of playgrounds as drug zones, a lack of community promotion, and a shifting interest to basketball and football. Even Major League Baseball finds this trend disturbing, as it may partly account for the decline of African-Americans attending games and playing organized and professional baseball.

A local professional baseball franchise has contributed funds for regenerating interest of inner-city youth in baseball. The baseball franchise is working in tandem with city government to restore baseball fields and to solicit volunteer organizers and coaches. Working at the grass roots level, your task is to train a group of speakers to visit urban elementary and middle schools to rekindle interest in organized youth baseball. Concentrating on various nonverbal factors (dress, proxemics, artifacts, oral tone, etc.), how would you advise speakers to integrate nonverbal elements as attention-gaining complements to the presentation? Be imaginative and resourceful.

ISSUES FOR DEBATE AND DISCUSSION

Debate stimulates a wide-ranging analysis of issues. Debating aspects of social volunteerism reflects our goal of melding classroom pedagogy with community concerns. This process joins theory with spirited discussions of the ethics and efficacy of community service. Community service issues worthy of debate are listed below. Your class may add to the list. Treat the issues as debate resolutions or as questions for class discussion. Your instructor has the option of choosing from a variety of discussion or debate formats.

1. Service-learning should be a required part of high school and college education.
2. An internship in the private sector provides more benefit than community service to promoting professional growth.

3. Communication skills are better learned through community involvement than through classroom studies.
4. Service devoted to causes of social justice, the environment, or public health is worthier than service devoted to the arts.
5. Service-learning should/should not include volunteer work for religious organizations.
6. Financial compensation for students engaged in service-learning diminishes the spirit of service.
7. Performing community outreach for a private corporation is/is not consistent with the principles of service-learning.

ALTERNATE MESSAGE FORUMS FOR COMMUNITY ACTIVISM

Capturing and holding the attention of an audience is a challenge for all speakers. In this chapter thus far, we have presented a range of theories and methods of persuasion to transform speeches into effective advocacy messages. In the following section, we present alternate forms of message design and delivery that can embolden service-learning messages to successfully captivate and motivate audiences to think, feel, and respond passionately to community issues.

Images have the power to stimulate the imagination and evoke emotion. The adage, "A picture is worth a thousand words," coined in 1927 by publicist Fred R. Barnard, lays claim to the notion that images are richly symbolic, providing an abundant source of inspiration for the formulation of evocative messages.

Advertisers use images to promote everything from dairy products to financial services. The California Milk Advisory Board's advertisements feature "happy cows" grazing in sunlit, verdant pastures. These images evoke favorable feelings about cows, which ultimately translates into good feelings about the product, California cheese. In a recent advertisement for on-line investing, Charles Schwab incorporates the image of a knight on a white horse to capture the imagination of its audience.

Images can have a direct relationship to the message, as in the case of the cows in the advertisements for California cheese. They can also be allegorical, used to represent or symbolize an idea or principle. The Charles Schwab commercial uses the image of the knight ironically to demonstrate the disparity between fantasy and the pragmatic reality of investing funds wisely.

Integrating images into service-learning messages is a powerful way to bring your message to life for your audience. An original photograph, graphic, or painting can serve as the foundation for formulating and strengthening your message. Although advertisers often incorporate visual images with text, it is not always necessary that your audience have direct access to your image. A compelling image chosen to literally or figuratively inspire your service-learning message can inspire evocative language that will animate your message. Brainstorming descriptive words and emotions resonating from the image is an important first step in the process of integrating an image into your message. Using the selected photograph, graphic, or artifact as a visual aid may enhance your message and heighten the connection between the image and the issue, yet your language alone should capture the essence of the image, thereby creating a picture in the mind's eye of your audience. Much like the astronomy major achieved in motivating high school students to pursue science in college by speaking about the celestial wonders revealed by the Hubbel telescope. Without visual aids, he described distant images of "luminous fountains, cascading streams of light, and pulsing orbs."

Choosing a visual image to energize a service-learning message is a creative endeavor that may evolve in a variety of ways. While constructing your message, you may recall a familiar photograph, picture, or painting that connects in an abstract or concrete way with your topic. Or you may need to set aside time to peruse magazines, art history books, or web sites for images that complement your topic.

Once you have located an image, you will want to spend time observing it and developing a list of descriptive words and emotions the image inspires. As you record your impressions of the image, you should begin to think of ways in which the evocative language you have generated might add dimension to your message. You may choose to integrate the image thematically throughout the entire speech, creating a richly-textured advocacy message that is both inspirational and motivating to your audience. Alternately, you may decide to use the image as an attention device, piquing the interest of your audience by creatively drawing them into your topic.

The following service-learning message provides an example of how you might integrate a painting from one of the old masters into a persuasive message designed to recruit volunteers:

While surfing an on-line gallery one Sunday afternoon, I came upon a painting by Caravaggio entitled The Boy with the Basket of Fruit. The face of this boy, flushed and full of uncertainty, captivated me. His eyes are honest and reflect vulnerability. This boy with the basket shows a willingness to be known as he offers his fruit to the viewer; a bountiful basket of shiny apples, red grapes, and golden peaches.

As I gazed into the face of the boy in this centuries-old painting, I imagined the face of a first-time volunteer for Project Open Hand looking into the eyes of a homebound person for the very first time, presenting a hot meal or a bag of nutritious fresh foods.

Project Open Hand is a non-profit organization that provides nutritious meals and groceries to people in need. Established in 1985 by Ruth Brinker, a retired grandmother, Project Open Hand initially provided home-delivered hot meals to seven people living with HIV/AIDS. Today, Project Open Hand delivers hot or frozen meals to over 2,000 people who are homebound due to illnesses of all kinds, and serves hot lunches to senior citizens at 21 sites throughout San Francisco.

Project Open Hand receives funding from charitable foundations, the state and local government, and personal donations from people like me. It is the volunteers, however, who are the lifeblood of the organization. Project Open Hand needs 125 volunteers a day, 7 days a week, to slice and dice food, pack bags of groceries, deliver meals to the homebound, and serve hot lunches to seniors. Volunteers at Project Open Hand receive many rewards for their efforts and I would like to share with you some of the ways in which each of you might personally benefit from becoming a volunteer.

Volunteers at Project Open Hand share a sense of purpose. On a recent broadcast of ABC Salutes, several Project Open Hand volunteers indicated that they initially volunteered thinking they were going to give something to people in need, only to discover that they were getting something in return. One volunteer indicated "volunteering at Project Open Hand is not only a way for you to give back to your community, it is a way for you to become part of your community." Volunteers at Project Open Hand make lifelong friendships; not only with other volunteers, but also with the people they serve. One volunteer named Manuel De La Cruz said that volunteering at Project Open Hand delivers "instant gratification," claiming that volunteering fills his heart with love.

Volunteering requires you to become vulnerable; vulnerable to the people you meet and the diverse perspectives you encounter. Whether you find yourself answering telephones, making calls requesting support, cooking up love in one of their kitchens, or working on the front-line talking with and getting to know the people you serve, Project Open Hand calls on you to open your mind and your heart.

I encourage you to find out just how rewarding volunteering can be. You can attend a one-hour volunteer orientation meeting at 6:00 p.m. every Wednesday evening at 730 Polk Street, or you can find out more about the organization by visiting the web site at www.openhand.org. Find out how you can spread good will and good food to the homebound of San Francisco. As Ruth Brinker, the founder of Project Open Hand, says, 'There is no greater feeling in the world than to bring food to someone who really needs it.' Like Caravaggio's gentle boy with the basket of fruit, Project Open Hand invites you to touch the lives of others, providing nourishment for the body as well as the soul.

Class Activity

Locate a visual image that appeals to you and inspires a topic for a persuasive community service message. As you observe the image, develop a list of descriptive words and emotions that resonate from the image. Write an introduction to a persuasive speech using the image as an attention device to capture the interest of your listeners and serve as a foundation for integrating the image into your message.

Class Activity

The use of compelling imagery may have multiple applications. One student used Picasso's painting, *The Old Guitarist,* to craft the following introduction, conclusion and application of Schwartz's theory of resonance (using symbols to connect to common audience experiences) for a speech on homelessness:

Haven't you seen someone like this solitary, withered figure huddled in a doorway as the blue-violet shadows of evening fell? Painted in 1903, Picasso's 'The Old Guitarist," could depict homelessness in our own era. The painting's somber blue shades connect us to the melancholy of the homeless.

Was this man once a promising young music student? There still remains a touch of fragile nobility in the way he caresses his guitar. This image begs the question, who hare the homeless? From what backgrounds do they come? How did they become society's outcasts? Picasso came to know the homeless of Barcelona. Today, I will provide you with surprising answers to the question, "Who are the homeless on our own city streets?

Continuing the thread of resonance with audience experience, the speaker redisplayed Picasso's image to support the speech's conclusion.

In the violet-blue shadows of evening, when a kindred soul of the old guitarist seeks refuge in a doorway, head listing, body slumped from fatigue and despair, don't avert your eyes. The man or woman may hold a cup, rather than a guitar, but examine the weather-beaten face with its life-map of deeply furrowed lines. Think of this person as someone who once emitted a brighter light, maybe a rambunctious fourth-grader running in school yard, or even a brilliant guitarist in a music conservatory. Keep your assumptions and your heart open.

The use of compelling imagery in an introduction and conclusion can create a focused immediacy, encouraging an audience to emotionally connect with the topic. The example with Picasso's *The Old Guitarist* puts a specific human face on the subject of homelessness. The body of a speech expands the scope of the topic. Working in small groups and using the above introduction and conclusion inspired by Picasso's image, brainstorm and then outline an approach for developing a body for this speech on homelessness. To help design an outline for the body of the speech, consider the following:

1. Refine the specific purpose of the speech.
2. Determine the context and audience for the speech.
3. Devise transitions to connect the introduction and conclusion to the body of the speech.
4. After determining the main points of the body, determine what pattern of organization would best present your ideas (e.g., problem-solution, cause-effect, chronological ordering).
5. Consider additional concepts/theories of persuasion that might enhance the persuasive qualities of the body (e.g., credibility, diverse evidence, human needs theory).

Analyzing Current Public Service Announcements for Examples of Effective Persuasion

NBC's public service campaign, *The More You Know,* uses celebrities to deliver important messages about social issues ranging from child abuse and mentoring to parental involvement with schools. These public service announcements (PSAs), specifically designed to capture the attention of parents or children, air during primetime and Saturday morning programming.

The More You Know Campaign has received several national awards for excellence in public service announcements and can serve as an exemplar for service-learning messages created and presented at the local or community level.

Tony Schwartz's resonance theory, which focuses primarily on electronically mediated communication, suggests that in order for an advertisement or commercial to induce the "desired learning or behavioral effect" (Schwartz, 1973, p. 24), it must resonate with the information or experience stored in the minds of the individual listener or viewer. Likewise, John O'Toole, former chairman of the board for the advertising agency Foote, Cone, and Belding, believes that the consumer should be at the center of the advertising process; in other words, advertisements should develop a "personal, one-to-one relationship" (O'Toole, 1980, p. 82) with members of the audience. According to O'Toole, there is a significant difference between directing a message to "people" versus "a person" (O'Toole, 1980, p. 83). The challenge for advertisers, states O'Toole, is to make a specific statement to an individual, while at the same time appealing to a large audience. Schwartz and O'Toole agree that consumers must recognize some part of themselves in the advertisement.

The More You Know recently produced a PSA targeted for parents that addresses the issue of prejudice and tolerance. The text for this PSA (provided below) illustrates Schwartz and O'Toole's theories regarding the effectiveness of connecting with the audience on a personal level.

> *You're a good parent. You help with homework. You taught your child not to say those four-letter words. But if you're not careful you might teach them the most offensive four-letter word of all: HATE. It's so easy to teach hate you might not even know you're doing it, because when you make those comments about the person with the different- colored skin or religion, or the person who speaks a different language, you're teaching your child to hate. Hate is a four-letter word. So is love. Which word will you teach your child?*

This PSA effectively addresses individuals rather than a collective group of people. The carefully crafted message is designed to resonate with parents by connecting with familiar activities, such as helping their children with homework.

Class Activity

Literacy affects every aspect of our personal, social, and economic lives. It affects our self-esteem, our relationships with others, our ability to participate in the community, and the ability to support our families and ourselves. ProLiteracy America helps adults learn to read, write, and speak English proficiently in order to lead more productive and meaningful lives. The success of the ProLiteracy program depends upon public awareness about literacy, and the recruitment of tutors who are willing to work with learners once or twice a week for a minimum of 2 hours.

Work in teams of 4 or 5 to prepare a 30 to 60-second public service announcement designed for broadcast on your college radio station. Use Schwartz and O'Toole's theories for connecting with individual listeners to recruit tutors for ProLiteracy America. Begin by researching pertinent facts about the impact of illiteracy.

Oral Interpretation of Literature for Social Activism

Literature puts into words thoughts and impressions of life that we previously may have been unable to articulate. It opens our minds to perspectives of life that are different from our own; helping us to broaden our horizons and add new dimensions to our understanding of life. Through the written word, writers and poets share their understanding and questions about life, allowing readers to develop their own philosophical, spiritual, and social attitudes (Brooks, Bahn, & Okey, 1975). The author's ideas, coupled with the reader's experiences and perspectives, create a unique interpretation of life that adds depth to the intended or unconscious meaning of the original work.

The interpretation of literature in public speaking predates recorded history. Oral recitation was used in ancient Greece to communicate laws, to teach, and to entertain. The minstrels and rhapsodes of ancient Greece not only entertained and inspired their audiences, they also fulfilled an important role in the community by passing on the history of the people from one generation to the next (Brooks, Bahn, & Okey, 1975).

Literature rich with imagery can be used as a foundation for your message. In *The Communicative Act of Oral Interpretation* (1975), Brooks, Bahn, and Okey suggest that the oral interpreter is capable of breathing life into written words through the vivid and accurate use of voice and body. Through vocal and physical cues, the oral interpreter can identify the significance and relationship of symbols. Linking a piece of poetry or prose to a community service message allows the speaker to create an intellectual and emotional connection between the author, the literature, the social issue or cause, the speaker, and the audience.

Lewis Hershey (1988) claims that "rhetorical and poetical language are interdependent forms of discourse" (p. 264). Hershey states that "poetical language forms argue for ways of seeing, thinking, and feeling that are different from the products of cause-effect or problem-solution reasoning" (p. 263). It follows that poetry, prose, or drama may serve as an alternative form of evidence or argument for your community service message.

Langston Hughes' poem *Dream Deferred* is rich with images that conjure up sensory responses. If, for example, we integrated Hughes' poem into a service-learning message for the Stay-in-School program sponsored by the U.S. Department of State, this poem could emphasize the potential consequences of postponing our dreams and aspirations:

Dream Deferred
By Langston Hughes
What happens to a dream deferred?
Does it dry up
 Like a raisin in the sun?
 Or fester like a sore –
And then run?
Does it stink like rotten meat?
Or crust and sugar over –
Like a syrupy sweet?

Maybe it just sags
Like a heavy load.

Or does it just explode?

Hughes' poem offers a paradox of possibilities ranging from devastation to hope. If woven into a message designed to encourage students to stay in school, this poem could lend credibility to our cause by stimulating our senses and evoking strong emotions regarding the negative consequences of deferring our dreams. Presented from an alternate perspective, Hughes' poem could be merged into a message delivered on behalf of Sigma Theta Tau International, the Honor Society of Nursing. The poem could easily lend credibility and life to a speech for reentry students delivered to a group of single-mothers who need encouragement to fulfill their long-forgotten dreams of becoming nurses.

Class Activity

Using Langston Hughes' poem *Dream Deferred* as the blueprint for a community service message, write a persuasive speech encouraging students to stay in school, or a persuasive speech to single-mothers encouraging them to return to school in pursuit of their dreams of becoming nurses.

Consider the strategic placement of the poem within the structure of your speech. You may consider including the poem in the introduction thereby establishing a theme that can unite the body and conclusion of your speech. When delivering your message, recite the poem with a reinforcing style that highlights the particular interpretation you want your audience to embrace.

What We Can Learn from the Lyceum and Chautauqua Movements of the 19th Century:

In 19th century America, the one-person shows of the Lyceum and Chautauqua circuits showcased writers and platform lecturers. Poets, preachers, politicians, novelists, and lecturers recited their own works, as well as the works of others (Gentile, 1989). Charles Dickens, Edgar Allen Poe, James Murdock, Ralph Waldo Emerson, Henry David Thoreau, and Oliver Wendell Holmes are just a few famous figures who delivered one-person performances and readings in these 19th century forums.

Helen Potter, celebrated throughout the late 1870s and 1880s as "Queen of the Lyceum" (Gentile, 1989), was known for adding a theatrical approach to platform reading. She created accurate impersonations of famous people, using their text to add credibility and potency to her platform presentations. Potter wore elaborate costumes and strived to embody the physical and vocal features particular to her subjects. Gentile (1989) refers to Potter's work as the "recycling or refertilization of inspiration" (p. 43). Among Potter's impersonations were Abraham Lincoln's *Gettysburg Address,* Elizabeth Cady Stanton's *Declaration of Rights,* Susan B. Anthony's speech *On Trial for Voting,* and Oscar Wilde's lecture *Art.* Leland Powers, another distinguished Lyceum and Chautauqua performer, was known for his ability to portray a variety of characters with nothing more than a change of voice and manner.

In our sophisticated age of electronic media, the classic "low-tech" performance style of the Lyceum and Chautauqua can still serve as a compelling device for community activism. The dramatic interpretation of historical figures now often falls under the category of performance art. As illustrated in the following section, this classic dramatic medium remains a creative avenue for social and political advocacy.

Many of you have probably heard of the debate within Congress, environmental protection circles, and the oil industry concerning the expansion of oil drilling in Alaska. Specifically, the debate has focused on drilling in the Artic National Wildlife Refuge (the ANWR). While the main thrust of this debate has been in arenas, such as Congress, television news and talk shows, political rallies, and the Internet, several performance artists have barrowed a page from the Lyceum and Chautauqua in an attempt to halt drilling in the ANWR. Upon examination of these artistic approaches to environmental protection, one can see established theories of persuasion in action.

John Muir is an iconic figure in the ecology movement. Spearheading the founding of our national parks and the Sierra Club, and writing poetically of the grandeur of America's wilderness, Muir remains a timeless voice for the preservation of our natural inheritance. Muir's continuing influence has encouraged performance artists to dramatically recreate his persona in stage performances, directly speaking the elegant prose he contributed to American literature.

A contemporary drama student, performing in the tradition of the Lyceum and Chautauqua, delivered a dramatic performance in a community theatre in Palo Alto, California in Muir-like costuming, interpreting the naturalist's literary description of pristine 19th century Alaska. The performer juxtaposed Muir's own account of an unspoiled Alaska against projected images of the ANWR scarred by oil development.

The performer opened his presentation stating, "When he was in his fifties, John Muir's life took an unforeseen career path. The very shy and private mountaineer became a very public man, required to make speeches and lead in social affairs."

He continued with Muir's words, describing the region now called the ANWR.

The majestic cliffs and mountains forming the canyon walls display endless variety of form and sculpture, and are wonderfully adorned and enlivened with glaciers and waterfalls, while throughout almost its whole extent the floor is a flowery landscape garden, like Yosemite. The most striking features are the glaciers, hanging over the cliffs, descending the side canyons and pushing forward to the river, greatly enhancing the wild beauty of all the others…I love getting acquainted with the trees, especially the beautiful spruce and silver fir, the flower gardens and great grassy caribou pastures…

Shifting to his own words, the performer offered,

But the velvety caribou pastures Muir so eloquently described will be littered with a crisscross of pipelines and industrial machinery if the current administration in Washington has its way with the ANWR. If we are to honor John Muir and preserve our natural inheritance we must, like the title of a famous Muir speech, 'Watch, Pray and Fight.'

From the perspective of service-learning, the dramatic interpretation of Muir's literature illustrates persuasive strategies grounded in cultural mythology and narrative impact. The interpretation of Muir and Muir's writings embodies a classic American myth, the "Wisdom of the Rustic." This myth is expressed in the unsullied wisdom of the backwoods character, like a young Abraham Lincoln splitting rails by day and studying literature by evening candlelight, honing an authentic and natural intellect.

A wilderness explorer, a student of Thoreau and Emerson, and an eloquent recorder of nature, Muir personifies the qualities of the rustic sage. With our ever expanding population and shrinking wilderness, the appeal of this classic American myth endures.

The classic storytelling tradition of the Lyceum and Chautauqua also illustrates the potential of the narrative to transport audiences. Several theorists base their work on the idea that drama or story is the most powerful metaphor that humans use to persuade and explain events (Larson, 2003). We use stories to help construct and make sense of events. Narrative style possesses a closer relationship to everyday experiences, making comprehension more natural than may occur from argumentative and logical reasoning styles, and is the easiest genre to recall. Audiences in the sway of an artistically formed narrative are motivated to search for both immediate and global connections to the theme. Muir's description of the pristine 19th Century Alaskan landscape creates a ready incentive to conjure contrasting images of degradation from future oil development.

Enduring narratives also provide vehicles for coalescing ideological communities. Thus the ecologically minded audience likely attracted to a dramatization of John Muir, the man and his words, are promising adherents to an appeal to preserve the landscape he described in his literary rhapsodies. Even a less ecologically minded audience would probably better attend to a narrative painted by an American icon than they would to a strident argument posed by a contemporary environmental activist. The skillful interpreter of Muir and his philosophy still provides compelling testimony for the preservation of our natural endowment, including the pristine ANWR.

Class Activity

In small groups brainstorm various stories, scenes, or dialogues from literature, theatre, or film that express themes of social need. Discuss how a dramatic interpretation of a scene from one of these works could be presented as a means for promoting a contemporary social or community cause. What presentational format would best enhance the interpretation of the intended message? After deliberating for 30 minutes, each group reports its ideas to the class.

Crafting the Efficient Snapshot Speech

Public forums often impose strict time limits on speakers. Such constraints demand that speakers resourcefully manage time, as in the case of a public hearing with an open microphone format that limits speakers to two-minute statements.

In such a circumstance, this author planned a 2-minute speech before a park commission considering levying a $5.00 admission fee to a botanical garden, a 40 acre urban oasis of exotic gardens, tranquil woods, and artistically landscaped ponds and brooks, all free of car traffic. This bucolic retreat was more a haven for local residents than for visiting tourists. I feared that the imposition of an admission fee would deny many city residents access to their treasured refuge.

But this public forum posed a communication challenge. How can one significantly affect public policy when allotted only a two-minute statement? What techniques of message design and theory can provide a short speech with lasting impact on decision-makers?

Speaking against the proposed admission fee, I focused my speech on the daily activity surrounding a simple park bench that commanded a magnificent view of the gardens. This anchoring point was viewed through the chronology of a typical day, an account of the visitors who regularly used this bench to relax, read, talk and enjoy the serenity.

I opened my presentation by asking, "What would a still camera focused on a single bench for an entire day reveal about visitors to the botanical gardens?" I then guided the board members through a daily chronology. Here follow a few excerpts.

Hearing the garden gates scrap open at 8:00 AM, a gaggle of geese scurry across the lawn to greet their fair lady who sits regally upon the bench. To the outside world this monarch of the gardens is a bag lady. But within her plastic garbage bag of worldly possessions she carries a loaf of bread, her daily offering for her feathered subjects…

At 9:00 Mrs. Jenkins, a retired elementary school teacher, a reading specialist who still tutors 5th and 6th graders every week, sits on the bench and opens her novel. She will read for an hour, every few minutes stopping to admire the grove of plum trees in spring blossom…

At noon a harried young mother claims the bench. Here she can allow her 9- month old twins to crawl about with no worry of car traffic. How she treasures this daily hour of calm...

The day's chronology of the park bench continues with a procession of eclectic occupants, like the four elderly men holding stemming cups of tea, speaking animatedly in Russian, debating politics and recalling boyhood memories.

Completing my chronology of this simple scene, I concluded with the following:

Let's fast forward by six month our view of the bench, after the admission fee you are considering today has been imposed. The Russian quartet, the young mother, Mrs. Jenkins, and the patroness of geese, are all absent. These once faithful garden regulars do not know each other and will not gather to collectively march with placards protesting the admission charge. Today I just wanted to tell their story of how a precious retreat would be taken from them.

As described earlier in this chapter, visually rich speech encourages an audience to co-create a message, as listeners reflexively internalize and complete images suggested by the speaker. Both the clarity of the message and the ability to retain it are enhanced, because listeners have helped to link imagery with argument. The use of a single scene in the preceding speech created a focused and time efficient design for a short statement, and presented an argument connected to tangible human characters. The strategy is simply to let a series of related and compelling snapshots tell a story and leave a vivid imprint. The proposal for the admission fee was defeated.

Guerrilla Media and Community Activism

A guerilla media campaign uses low-cost media to promote community causes. The concept offers a potential remedy to the view that influential media remain unavailable to the average person. Guerrilla media campaigns have succeeded in creating legislation, environmental awareness, and consumer rights (e.g., persuading the McDonald's Corporation to reduce wasteful packaging, recruiting volunteers to join literacy programs, increasing security on college campuses). In the spirit of service-learning, guerrilla media motivates activists to "Think globally, but act locally," encouraging students to undertake projects that positively affect their communities. Guerrilla Media also fosters the entrepreneurial dimension of service-learning, enabling a group to independently address a community need outside of the sponsorship of an established agency.

As an orientation to this unit, students should view the video, "Guerrilla Media," available in most college audio-visual libraries. The video features Tony Schwartz, considered the "Father of Guerrilla Media." With case study examples, Schwartz shows how common citizens can overcome media cost, indifference, and inaccessibility by resourcefully developing persuasive messages for radio, print, and telephone, inexpensively and effectively. Schwartz's principles are easily adaptable to e-mail and the Internet.

With its relatively modest production cost and audience reach, radio is often the guerrilla media activist's medium of choice. The 60-second public service announcement spot, (reinforced with widely distributed print material) is often the centerpiece of guerrilla media campaigns. A tape recorder with a good microphone can usually produce a radio quality message. Despite the short length of such messages, they typically exhibit the structure of the Monroe Motivated Sequence (see included sample text). Even though Schwartz does not employ Monroe's terminology, notice that in successive steps the sample messages create statements of attention, need, satisfaction, visualized results, and requested action. Because the message must be expressed concisely, time constraint requires the economic application of this model.

Schwartz's template for a guerrilla media message reflects classic rhetorical principles. He lists the following communication guidelines for the effective message:

1.   Audiences will listen to what involves them.

2. Aim campaigns at specific leaders and institutions. Don't associate a problem with nebulous factions like "oil industry." It's better to direct action against a CEO of a particular company. Schwartz contends that leaders are concerned about anything that may embarrass them in the public arena.

3. Ask yourself, "Whom are you trying to reach with your campaign?" Define your specific audience.

4. Ask yourself, "What do you want as a result? Do you want a change in attitudes or a particular action to take place?"

5. Start your message with a question to generate audience interest.

6. Conclude your message with clear directions for audience action (telephone number to call, address to contact, etc.).

7. Write like you speak. The guerrilla media message should have a direct, personal tone.

Sample Guerrilla Media Campaign

San Francisco, like many urban areas, grapples with problems of public transportation. College students are especially dependent upon the system and experience its full range of problems. A small group in my persuasion class directed their guerrilla media campaign at the city's trouble-filled municipal railway system. Included are extracts of their central campaign message, its organizational design, persuasive strategy, and instructor commentary. Note that the central message incorporates each step of the Motivated Sequence.

A. Gaining Attention (extract)

Mayor Brown, have you ever had to rely on Muni?
Have you ever rushed down the stairs off Market Street, dodging garbage and the homeless encampment?
Mayor Brown, have you ever frantically raced up to a change machine only to find it out of order?
And Tell me Mr. Mayor, have you ever tried to get basic information from an indifferent and irritated Muni agent?

B. *And by the way, have you ever stood 45 minutes waiting for Muni because the scheduled car was broken down?*
APPARENTLY NOT!

In this extract from the opening statement (produced on audiotape and intended for the college radio station), notice the rhythmic repetition of questions that invites audience response. The mayor is the singular target, as he made improvement of the Muni system a prime campaign issue. He faces the embarrassing consequences of not improving the system. Resonance theory is employed to evoke the common frustrations of any student who regularly uses the system.

C. Stating the Need (extract)
Because if you did, you would have replaced the 40 million dollars you cut from the Muni budget.
You would also have rehired the 200 mechanics that you let go. Had you known, you would repair the dozens of Muni cars that are broken down on any given day.
So Mayor Brown. Now that you know, what are you going to do about it!

Notice that the message maintains a direct, conversational tone. Problems are clearly and concisely stated.

D. Satisfaction of the Need (extract)
We are S.A.V.E. MUNI-Students Acting for a Viable, Effective Muni. We call upon you, Mayor Brown, to make Muni's problems the first agenda item at the Board of Supervisors meeting on May 1. We expect this meeting to be open to the public, and we expect our leaders to restore the 40 million dollars you cut from the Muni budget...

The group's acronym establishes a clear and appropriate organizational identity. The message also presents a precise, unambiguous solution.

E. Visualize Results (extract)
"Imagine a public transportation system that reliably gets people to work and students to class on time. Image a system that

tourists and senior citizens would not fear to ride…"

This extract illustrates the broad benefits of improving the railway system in a single composite picture.

F. Action Step
"If you are fed up with Muni and demand the transportation system we were promised, call Mayor Willie Brown's office at 987-6543. Call Now! Let's demand change? That number again is 987-6543."

The message calls for a clear, targeted and unified audience response. Too often persuasive messages generate enthusiasm, but fail to provide a clear path for action.

The studies of learning and attitude change theory have established that information retention and opinion change require message reinforcement. The guerrilla media project requires that groups design flyers or posters to complement the principle media spot. Exposure to the principle message makes attention to a flyer more likely. A passerby may recognize a bold poster headline or familiar acronym from the original radio message on the college station. The poster or flyer should exhibit the same qualities of attention gaining, conciseness, clarity, specific targeting, and clear action advocated in the radio spot.

Students are not powerless in the face of campus and local problems. Whether acting on the problems of parking, tuition and housing costs, public safety, or fund-raising, learning the methods of guerrilla media can provide students with the tools to improve their community.

References

Bennett, T. (1982). (Theories of the Media: Theories of Society." In Gurevtich R., Bennett, T., Curran, J., and Woollacott, J. (Eds.), Culture, Society and the Media. London: Methueun.

Boorstin, D.J. (1961). The Image: A Guide to Pseudo-events in America. New York: Harper and Row.

Brooks, K., Bahn, E., & Okey, L. L. (1975). *The Communicative Act of Oral Interpretation.* Boston: Allyn and Bacon.

Burke, K. (1960). A Grammar of Motives. Berkeley: University of California Press.

Eagley, A.H., & Chaiken, S. (1993). The Psychology of Attitudes. New York: Harcourt, Brace, Jovanovich.

Fishbein, M., Ajzen, I. (1975). Belief, Attitude, Intention, and Behavior: An Introduction to Theory and Research. Reading, MA: Addison Wesley.

Gentile, J. S. (1989). *Cast of One: One Person Shows from the Chautauqua Platform to the Broadway Stage.* Chicago: University of Illinois Press.

Hershey, L. (1988). The performance of literature as argument. *The Southern Speech Communication Journal, 53,* 259-278.

Howell, W.S., & Borman, E.G. (1988). The Process of Presentational Speaking. New York: Harper and Row.

Larson, Charles U. (1995). Persuasion: Reception and Responsibility. Belmont, CA: Wadsworth/Thomson Learning.

Larson, Charles (2003). *Persuasion: Reception and Responsibility.* Belmont, CA: Wadsworth Thomson Learning.

McLuhan, M. (1964). Understanding Media. New York: Signet.

O'Toole, J. (1980). *The Trouble with Advertising.* New York: Times Books.

Petty, R.E., & Cacioppo, J.T. (1986). Communication and Persuasion: Central and Peripheral Routes to Attitude Change. New York: Springer-Verlag.

Schwartz, T. (1973). The Responsive Chord. New York: Anchor

Zimbardo, P.G., & Leippe, M.R. (1991). The Psychology of Attitude Change and Social Influence. New York: McGraw-Hill.

CHAPTER 6

TRANSACTIONAL COMMUNICATION IN SERVICE ORGANIZATIONS

With increased telecommunications and use of the internet there is an information and transaction explosion in the work environment today that has altered the nature, scope, speed, and detail of data and contact with others. The environment and pace changes quickly and decisions that have far-reaching impact need to be made much more rapidly than ever before. Most often decisions are made based on the exchange of ideas, not as the direct result of a formal verbal presentation or memo. Presentations and written communication provide background material; it is in the give and take of transactional communications that agreements are made and individual leadership is developed. Understanding the contexts and mastering the techniques of transactional communications are critical skills in the work environment whether corporate, public or non-profit sectors.

Have you ever thought about a presentation or discussion, anticipating what might happen, and be surprised and caught unprepared by questions or comments that you did not know quite how to respond to? Many times we walk away from such encounters thinking, "If I had only thought to say this, or if I had only answered a different way, perhaps the outcome of the discussion would have been very different."

We all experience such feelings in our day-to day life. Because most discussion is unrehearsed, we sometimes feel unprepared to speak effectively. Yet, the ability to be an effective communicator in interactions is very important for success. The discomfort with the prospect for communication in organizational contexts is universal for many young adults. Yet, they are very comfortable in social interactions with their friends and classmates. Some of these same skills can be utilized in a more formal context and your ability to understand and be adept at interactive communications or what we are calling transactional communications will be important for your success in any future career that involves decision-making, team building, and problem-solving.

How important are these skills in today's public service and general workplace? A recent Wall Street Journal/Harris interactive survey among business recruiters ranked *communication, interpersonal skills, and the ability to work well within teams* as the three top attributes out of 24 skills for rating job applicants for management positions.[1]

These speech communication skills are just as valued in the global work environments in all sectors of the economy in which people will be working with information, concepts, and collaborative activities. In a recent report by the World Bank (2002) the most important new competencies that employers value in the knowledge economy, "...have to do with oral and written communications, teamwork, peer teaching, creativity, envisioning skills, resourcefulness, and the ability to adjust to change."[2]

Service learning is an excellent environment to improve these skills. This chapter is devoted to providing the student with a better understanding of the context and dynamics of transactional communications and techniques to improve your abilities to master transactional speaking using the service-learning environment as a context.

A DEFINITION OF TRANSACTIONAL COMMUNICATION IN PUBLIC SPEECH

In any organization where we work collaboratively, the purposeful interaction among people to make decisions and solve problems is the lifeblood for effectiveness---both for the individual and group. In a non-profit organization, whether it is a decision to fund raise more effectively, initiate a new program for the people served by the agency, or improve the current practices of the organization, transactional communication is the means for decision-making.

Here is a working definition:

---

[1] "The Top Business Schools, Playing Well With Others", by Ronald Alsop, Wall Street Journal, September 9, 2002
[2] "Constructing Knowledge Societies: New Challenges for Tertiary Education", The World Bank, Washington, DC, 2002

Transactional communication is a spontaneous interaction that leads to inform, affect an attitude, or persuade towards action. It is always intentional and purposeful.

A spontaneous interaction

Spontaneous is unrehearsed. Interaction is a dialogue between two or more people. The interchange in the dialogue is what determines success of the outcome. So transactional communication is akin to a negotiation, where there is "give and take" by the participants. In more formal public presentations and debate, there is also an interaction and response, but the intended point of view is usually not modified to accommodate the views of other participants.

Leads to inform, affect an attitude or persuade towards action

To lead is to direct others in interaction towards an outcome. The outcome of "informing" is to provide information that will be significant in the determination of either attitude or action. The outcome of "affecting attitude" is to have the other person positively inclined towards taking the action you are recommending. The outcome of "persuading towards action" is to actually elicit agreement for cooperation in an endeavor.

It is always purposeful and intentional

Communication in organizations must have an aim or something identified as an end to be attained. In this sense it is purposeful. By intentional we mean that it is done by design. There is a reason for the interaction and methods employed to obtain the desired outcome.

Case Study

The executive director of the film festival you are working for requests you to prepare a printed handout and verbal presentation to provide background on a series of films by the director Roman Polanski. Now imagine you meet the executive director in the hallway and she asks you what you thought about the Roman Polanski movie "The Pianist" and how it compares with some of his previous movies such as "Chinatown" and whether she should see the movie. Can you create an "off-the-cuff" response?

Here are some topics and examples of how you could respond using some comparisons between the two films (rent the movies on video or DVD and see them if you can):

• Violence and corruption as a metaphor for a malevolent society

In *Chinatown* physical violence by hired thugs and corrupt police manipulated by a wealthy real estate mogul, who wants to divert the water in Los Angles for his own financial benefit, is a microcosm of the corruption of power and money interests in American society and the negative societal and environmental consequences.

In the *Pianist*, the occupation of Poland by the Nazis unleashes a wave of Anti-Semitism, violence and oppression by the occupiers that change the lives of a family, community and nation, who are innocent victims. The veneer of civilization is stripped away and individuals choose to either profit from or resist the Nazi system. Individual people--- victims, bystanders, or oppressors----are revealed in their actions under stressful conditions.

• Identification with outsider protagonist anti-hero: the private eye detective in *Chinatown* and the Jewish concert pianist in *The Pianist*

The private eye detective played by Jack Nicholson slowly learns the details of the large scheme and the incestuous relationships between the woman who hired him and her family. Initially, he takes the case because of the money and his attraction to the character played by Faye Dunaway. He becomes personally motivated to uncover the truth. Through his actions to find the truth and his reaction to the revelations of the story, we as viewers identify with him and become emotionally involved in the film.

The pianist played by Adrien Brody is introduced as a character completely absorbed in his music; he lives with a loving extended family. As the Polish society transforms under the Nazi occupation to strip all of this away from him, he just focuses on survival. Through luck, the efforts of good-willed people and his own resourcefulness the character survives throughout the horrible Nazi occupation of Warsaw. In the end his love of music both saves him physically and restores his connection to civilization. We as viewers connect to the horror of the Nazi period through the portrayal of the individual story of this man.

Exercise

This can be an individual or a group exercise. Choose two examples of music, films, TV programs, or any other entertainment or art medium. Develop a five minute presentation in which you compare the two examples using two themes such as we have illustrated with the films *Chinatown* and the *Pianist*.

Individual and collective success

The mastery of transactional communications is crucial for both individual and collective success in a work environment. Success is often determined by the ability of individuals to persuade others to take cooperative action in an endeavor. Today's organizational environment necessitates cooperative efforts both within and between service organizations. The success of that cooperation is based upon the quality of the transactional interactions among the people who develop, direct and implement the efforts of those entities.

Imagine the amount of collaboration for an organization such as *Second Harvest*. They collect unused food from restaurants and catered events, which would normally be wasted, and distribute the food to homeless shelters and charitable organizations for the economically disadvantaged. They have to work with the donor organizations, the health department of cities, delivery vehicles, and the recipient organizations. Through this collaboration they are able to feed many people who would go hungry with good food that would be wasted.

Contexts: The meeting, informal discussion, phone, e-mail

Here are several of the most common settings for transactional communications.

The Meeting for Formal Discussion

Usually an agenda is proposed and topic areas agreed to for discussion. Often someone may be called upon to provide a report, formal presentation or background on what is to be discussed. Sometimes the topic may be to solve a particular problem or meet a new situation. After this preliminary there is open impromptu discussion. This is the core of the meeting where analysis of the problem and alternative solutions are discussed and agreed upon. Usually, most productive meetings take no more than one hour to achieve the objectives. The skill is in preparing and running the meeting to be focused, productive, and consensual.

The Encounter for Informal Discussion

Most transactional communication in an organization occurs in the office or community setting encounter. This is usually a one-to-one or small group meeting that is informal. The communication is conversational, yet daily decisions are mostly concluded in this setting. The physical context is usually in someone's personal office space or in a field-work setting. There is rarely an agenda. The subject is most often based on a particular day-to-day situation or problem that needs to be resolved to proceed with the activities of the organization.

The Telephone, Video/Audio Conference Discussion

Frequently, people conduct transactional communications over the telephone or conference call. Phone conversations tend to be shorter and more focused than informal face to face meetings. Often the phone is used to clarify information and understandings, provide a briefing on an event.

E-Mail

It is hard to believe that e-mail has not always existed as preferred medium for communications. How did we ever live without it? E-mail has become the preferred method of communication to confirm appointments, summarize discussion and recap meetings, propose actions---in brief; it has become the default method of communications for busy people. As a transactional communications tool, e-mail does provide a platform for quick and effective discourse. However, it is asynchronous. Unlike face-to-face, phone and video conference, e-mail exchange does not occur in real time interaction. You can read your e-mail in the morning and answer it in the evening or the next day with no non-verbal or iterative interaction. Be aware that e-mail is a written record of a conversation and can be forwarded to infinite numbers of people. The chatty style typified in e-mail correspondence belies its powerful place in the modalities of communication as ever more people utilize it as the preferred means of communication in the organizational workplace.

PRINCIPLES AND TECHNIQUES FOR SUCCESSFUL TRANSACTIONAL COMMUNICATIONS

The ability to conduct good transactional communications is an art that does take years of experience to cultivate. However, it can be learned. Once an individual has incorporated the basic principles, then with practice it does become easier and eventually becomes instinctual. Listen to a good impromptu speaker. It appears effortless. In the public policy sphere just observe Colin Powell or Bill Clinton who are each masters of transactional communications. On TV, observe Charlie Rose on PBS channels as he interviews in seemingly effortlessly conversational style high profile people in the arts, cinema, business, literature and government.

Exercise

Tune into the Charlie Rose Show on PBS or Brian Lamb on C-Span and observe how they question, listen and converse with their guests. Write down the techniques you observe and then practice those techniques yourself in role-playing discussions with your class-mates.

Here are several open-ended questions you can observe professional interviewers such as Charlie Rose or Brian Lamb utilize to open up more intimate conversation with a guest celebrity. Try them yourself with a class partner and pretend you are interviewing a prominent service sector personality such as Kim Gandy, President of NOW (National Organization of Women), the largest organization of feminist activists in the United States. NOW has 500,000 contributing members and 550 chapters in all 50 states and the District of Columbia. To learn more for the purposes of the interview check out the NOW website www.now.org

Questions for the interview:

1. Tell me what you were trying to accomplish by: writing this book, directing this movie, choosing this course of action, etc.

2. Who are the people who most influence you and what did you learn from them?

3. What are the most significant things you learned while working on this project?

4. People who know you tend to say you are a (serious artist, open-hearted, etc). Do you agree with what they say and why do you think they say this about you?

Setting objectives

While transactional communications may be less formal than traditional public speaking and debate, it does require discipline and preparation. Being able to effectively make statements and respond to questions requires a good understanding of the context of the situation, what is required of you, recall of facts, and an anticipation of questions and comments. These four objectives of any transactional communication are usually combined: inform, affect an attitude, persuade towards action, and build personal credibility. Decide which ones you will seek to achieve before you begin to speak.

Inform

Sometimes information or facts are the only things required. Suppose an executive director requests you to provide the latest results in a volunteer recruitment effort or a briefing on what happened in a town council meeting related to the organization's proposal for a playground in a public park. Then, all you need provide is a simple answer with one or two facts.

Example: "The event achieved our goal of recruiting ten new volunteers for the library literacy program. Of the ten who volunteered, five were young adults, which was the demographic group we most sought to recruit."

Example: "The town council meeting went very well. The parents who spoke for the project were articulate and passionate about the project. Our recruitment efforts for turnout for the meeting were successful. There were 42 adherents for the project in attendance with no one speaking to oppose the project."

Notice in each of these examples the use of facts and figures and the positioning of this supporting evidence to provide a conclusion about the success of the effort.

Affect an Attitude to Persuade

Transactional communication may employ persuasive techniques to affect an attitude. If you are trying to interest someone in the important goals of a community organization, then the structure of your communication will be different than the briefing to inform.

Example #1: "Our library literacy program has proven to be successful. We work with adults who are functionally illiterate. With six months of two hours of classes once a week with homework, we have achieved functional literacy with 85% of the people who complete the course. So, with the proven success of our programs well established, would you be interested in becoming involved with our organization?"

Example #2: "Playgrounds in public parks provide children with safe, happy environments to exercise outdoors and just have fun together. Playgrounds help young children form a sense of community outside of their own family and school. I remember spending many hours of fun with my friends on swings, seesaws and monkey bars. Do you have similar happy childhood memories in playgrounds? If yes, would you be willing to help us to make playgrounds more attractive in our community, so a new generation will have those same kinds of experiences that we share?"

Notice that in affecting an attitude there is an initial appeal in the first example to establish the credibility for success of the program, while in the second example there is an appeal to experiences we share as children. In both cases, we are requesting the recipient of the transactional communication to agree to become involved. This permission by the recipient then leads to the appeal for action.

Persuade Towards Action

Convincing a decision-maker to accept a recommendation or join in an action is an important purpose of transactional communication. How persuasive we are will often determine whether an idea, program, or course of action gets adopted and whether we can positively affect the course of action for our organizations. Persuasion is as critical for non-profit organizations as it is in the corporate business environment.

Example #1: "We request our community Rotary Club adopt the Library Literacy Program as the designated charity for its members this year. Our program changes lives positively in our community by giving adults the tools of literacy so they can lead more productive and happier lives for themselves, their families and the community. Every five hundred dollars donated by the Rotary Club will enable a functionally illiterate adult to read and thereby change a life. Please agree to our appeal to adopt our cause as your designated charity."

Example #2: "We request the city to build the playground designed for this park as part of next year's budget. Our parent group has acquired 500 signatures in our community in support of the park and our group has enlisted the local nurseries to donate the flowers and shrubs to beautify the space. The $100,000 required for the permits, construction and reports has already been budgeted in the community redevelopment plan. All we need is the approval of the city council to go ahead with the project as proposed. Please vote affirmatively on the proposal so the children in our community will have their playground to enjoy when school lets out next June"

Notice that persuasive communication provides the recommended action and the rationale for the listener to take that action. It is useful to provide the benefit of the action as part of the request.

Build Personal Credibility

We attempt to build our credibility through transactional communication. Credibility simply means the willingness of others to listen to and respect what we have to say. Credibility must be earned; it is not automatically given just because someone has a job title or is responsible for a project. In your own experience at school there are probably teachers who possess more credibility than others with students.

Many students feel quite intimidated in professional job interviews when they make the transition from school to careers. Your service in non-profit organizations provides a very powerful source of credibility to a prospective employer. Remember, employers are looking for people to hire who will be dependable and solve problems. Your student experience in the non-profit service sector can provide such credibility.

Example: "While in school I worked as an intern in our community library literacy program. During my senior year in college I was part of a team that developed a proposal that was adopted by our community Rotary Club. That program raised $20,000, which enabled 40 illiterate adults in our community to learn to read. In addition, I helped to recruit 10 new volunteer teachers from our community, half of whom were fellow college students. Through this experience I worked collaboratively with the business community leaders. I believe this has helped me prepare for the position I am interviewing for today."

Preparation Techniques

One of the ironies of effective transactional communications is that a seemingly effortless response to a question, or posing a thoughtful question or statement "off-the cuff", is often the result of practiced discipline. Indeed, it is the mental preparation and ability to call upon facts, information, insights, and relevant points in a concise and coherent manner that truly distinguishes a good communicator. Just as a well trained basketball athlete and team will assess the court and have plays rehearsed to meet opportunity, the good transactional speaker will seize the moment and make a comment or respond to a question that will "score" points for credibility and leadership in community workplace interactions.

Perhaps the most important and effective technique to improve your ability as an impromptu speaker is to develop the habit of taking five to ten minutes of quiet preparation time before a meeting to prepare yourself for statements and responses you will make to anticipated questions and comments. The person who comes best prepared has a better chance to lead a group to agreement and decisive action.

Here are several steps to improve your abilities:

Anticipate questions: Before meeting with people in either an office or out in the field write down statements you will make and questions you can anticipate from other participants. After each statement and question write down two or three proof points (include data and information) to support your statements.

Statement: A literacy program is a cost effective way to improve the economic well-being of people who are functionally illiterate.

Proof points:

- It only takes six months of classes to achieve functional literacy for life.

- Trained volunteers supervised by a training coach can teach a person to be literate for less than $500, including the cost of books and materials.

- The earning power of a literate person is twice as high as an illiterate person: on average at least $10,000 a year more in earnings.

Anticipated questions (preparation for answers):

- If you received more funding could you increase the number of people you successfully teach? (Are there sufficient volunteers and people signing up for classes?)
- What is the success rate of completion for those who start the program? (Have statistics on the percentage of those who register and complete the class.)
- Among which populations are you most or least successful? (Track participants by gender, age, ethnicity, and other relevant factors to report meaningful differences within the total population served.)
- How many volunteer teachers do you have? How long does it take to train them? How many people on average does each volunteer train? (This information should be readily available from an analysis of the program.)
- Do you find that literacy benefits areas of a person's life besides economic enhancement? If yes, in what ways? (Have anecdotal stories of people whose lives have improved for their families, mental health, and law abidance.)

Have information at your fingertips

Create files and summaries of information. This will enable you to "put your fingers" on the right information when needed. It is also useful to memorize insightful information that can be used in particular contexts:

"Functional literacy doubles earning power."

"Literacy halves the likelihood of incarceration among young adult males 16-30 years old."

"Every dollar donated to adult literacy programs is leveraged ten times over in the value of contributed volunteer hours."

You can organize information into categories such as:

- Funding sources and costs of providing services (financial data)
- Volunteer recruitment, training and retention
- Populations served and class participants

Write an outline

An outline serves like a map for communication. Just as you would not want to start a hike up a mountain or start a road trip without knowing the route or destination, so you should not start to say something without having a good idea of what you will say, how you will say it, and what main points you wish to make. An outline could be as simple as the opening, key statement, conclusion:

- Introduction: Anecdote of person who made transition from illiteracy to literacy and how it changed a life.
- Transition: Just as this one person benefited, imagine the impact on their own lives and society if more people could become literate.
- Key point: Adult literacy training is a great community investment (use information).
- Conclusion: Increased funding for a library program in adult literacy will enable us to serve those waiting to lead more productive lives and improve the well-being of our community.
- Action Step: Please adopt the Adult Literacy Program as your charity of choice this month for the Chamber of Commerce.

Active Listening and Encouraging Discussion

One of the most effective skill sets a good communicator can develop is the ability to encourage others to engage and come to agreement for consensus. Master these skills and you will be a leader and team-builder.

Use Active Listening in Problem-solving

Active listening is critical to good communications skills. It simply means listening to the other person's statements and questions, ensuring that you have heard them correctly and have qualified their concerns before proposing an agreement on a solution.

Case example

Just suppose you were personally involved in soliciting an individual for a large donation to your community youth orchestra. Your task is to increase the amount of money and the length of time for the gift of a subscriber to the symphony who has had their own children in the youth orchestra and who regularly attends performances of the Symphony (professional musicians) and the youth orchestra (teens who volunteer their time). Your objective in the transactional communication is to convince the donor to provide a multi-year gift ($5,000 to be given over 3-5 years) considerably higher than her/his annual subscription ($150) so the youth orchestra can hire staff, rent a hall, and provide additional rehearsals for performances. The prospective donor does not usually give so large a gift to charities. After explaining the importance of the youth symphony to the development of the individual teen musician and the benefit to the community of having a Youth Orchestra, you have asked the donor to consider the gift of $5,000 over a three year period and have explained how the money would be used. You know this donor cares about music, the youth symphony and is a generous person, but he may not be prepared to give so large a commitment to the Youth Orchestra.

Let's go through the discussion together and demonstrate the techniques of active listening in transactional communication. There are five steps that one can use in any combination (you need not use all five). Practice and develop your skills in active listening using these principles. You will be amazed at how much more persuasive you can be when you do not do all the talking!

1. Restate the question or statement of your counterpart so he/she is satisfied they have been heard

2. Qualify the concern by making explicit those problems or objections that are implicit in the communication
3. Establish criteria for solutions
4. Provide trial solutions
5. Come to agreement

Restate the question or statement of your counterpart so he/she is satisfied they have been heard.

Frequently, people have discussions based on what they thought they heard and missed the point that someone else has made or do not listen carefully for meaning. It is also reassuring to the other person if you exhibit that you have understood their point. People are more receptive of an alternate viewpoint if they feel they are heard.

Good TC skills: "I understand that $5,000 is a very large commitment. I know you care deeply about the youth orchestra and you said it gives you great satisfaction that your own children benefited so much from their music experience. A large donation of $5,000 is more than you are prepared to give. Is that correct?"

Qualify the concern by making explicit those problems or objections that are implicit in the communication

Sometimes people may raise an objection and not provide the reason why. They may not be fully aware of the different reasons or their own priorities unless they are openly and candidly questioned in a non-threatening way. The statement that $5,000 is too large of a donation than they are prepared to give can be examined and discussed. Depending on the answer or combination of answers, you can then get a better idea of what the real consideration is for the person and then address it.

Good TC skills: By your saying $5,000 is more money than you are prepared to give, do you mean?

- That is a higher level of financial support than you had previously considered giving to The Youth Orchestra?
- The money will not be used for good purposes?
- This is a larger amount than you believe other supporters with comparable income and lifestyle are giving?

- The amount is too much for you to commit to with the other financial obligations you have?
- You are not convinced the Youth Orchestra will continue to be viable and so do not want to make a large commitment to something that will not last?
- You have other charities to donate to that have a higher priority for your giving than the Youth Orchestra?

Establish criteria for solutions

    If you can get agreement on the person's needs to be satisfied before you propose a solution, there is a greater likelihood of achieving agreement. Assume that after discussion of the reasons for the objection, you determine that the person: cares about the youth orchestra as a primary cause for support in their charitable giving; believes the money will be put to good use; the Youth Orchestra will be viable for years to come; and concurs that other donors who are in their economic peer group are giving at the $5,000 level. The major problem for the donor is the financial burden of $5,000, when she/he has so many other demands for both their discretionary and charitable dollars. If this is the real problem, then you can offer criteria for coming up with a solution that addresses the donor's issues.

    Good TC skills: If we can find a way so the $5,000 gift to the Youth Orchestra can be more easily handled and not such a burden on your budget, would that make you more likely to consider that amount?

Provide trial solutions

    Once criteria are established for a solution, then there is implicit agreement that if the criteria are fulfilled, an agreement will be favorably concluded. Assume that the person is open to listening about alternatives that would be less burdensome.

    Good TC skills: There are several ways you could give the $5,000 and not "break your budget". Would you consider?

- A donation of appreciated stock, an old car, or other asset that is worth $5,000. If you donate an asset you would be able to take the full value of the tax deduction, but the Youth Orchestra would handle the paperwork and sale on your behalf.
- Spread the donation out over several years. If you could afford a $1,000 a year donation we could acknowledge your gift now, but receive payment over the time period you specify.

- If you will be selling a business, house, or any other major asset over the next year, could you designate the $5,000 gift as part of the sale and thereby lower your tax payment from the profits? You can commit the donation from future money that you will receive as a result of the sale.

Come to Agreement

A discussion about these options could provide the person with a satisfactory option to commit to the $5,000 donation. The likelihood of a successful agreement is greatly increased by the candid dialogue and active listening skills employed in these five steps. Clearly, being prepared with alternative solutions to the needs of your counterpart is part of good transactional communication. In this case, understanding several alternative ways for donors to make large gifts is necessary preparation for an active listening discussion.

Active listening may be the most effective tool you can employ for negotiation and consensus building. It requires not only hearing what the other person has said, but also consciously probing for solutions and points of agreement to reconcile differing viewpoints. It does not mean facile agreement or capitulation to opposing arguments. Rather, the active listener confirms what he has heard, questions assumptions, establishes shared criteria for solutions, and then suggests solutions that can satisfy the concerns or objections of the other parties in the discussion.

There are differing skill sets and objectives in negotiation and debate. Both approaches are appropriate, depending on the context and circumstance. The chart below details some of the distinguishing properties between them.

Table 1. Difference between debate and negotiation

Distinguishing Properties	Debate	Negotiation	Difference
Desired Outcome	Defeat the opponent	Arrive at a mutually beneficial agreement	Debate is win/lose Negotiation is win/win
Communication directed to	Third party referee or audience	Counterpart	Debaters talk at each other Negotiators talk with each other
Style	Adversarial	Conciliatory	Debate is combative Negotiation is collaborative
Listening objective	Find points of counterpart's weakness and gain advantage by exploiting them to improve your own position	Find points of agreement and build upon shared interests	Debaters listen to find fault Negotiators listen to find affirmation

Exercise:

Utilize these five steps in active listening with a work group or partner for the following persuasive circumstances:

1. Selecting a vacation destination based on a limited budget
2. Choosing a car to purchase (used or new, model, make, etc)
3. What job opportunities are most attractive to apply for after graduation

Be a Team-builder

Transactional communication in most work places is akin to negotiation. At work, people negotiate agreements with each other continually. Inherent is this process is the concept of teambuilding. Teambuilding strengthens the professional relationships of your co-workers by recognizing their viewpoints, concerns and contributions. Together, you develop decisions, programs and policies that will improve the performance of the group and the greater organization as a whole. A team-building leader encourages ideas, opens discussion, and resolves problems so the group can succeed. Here are some techniques in teambuilding that can improve your effectiveness in transactional communication.

Piggyback, Don't Refute

Often we have a tendency to argue and try and win a point with people by putting down their ideas and promoting our own. Much of our schooling orients us this way. Early in our education, we were taught to recognize, "What is wrong with this picture?" There might be 19 things right, but we were taught to identify what is wrong.

Piggy-backing is a different communications strategy. Rather than dispute an idea as we would in traditional debate, we can recognize what is right with the idea and then build upon it. This is a very powerful communications technique for bringing a group to consensus and having all involved feel a part of the solution.

Example:

Idea #1: "Let's increase ticket sales for the fund raising event by discounting the price of each ticket by 50%."

Piggyback on Idea #1: "I like the idea of promoting the event to increase ticket sales and make it more attractive for people to attend. I am concerned that discounting would reduce our profit from sales. Could we consider building more value into the event by increasing the number of prizes and getting one really attractive grand prize which we can advertise on our flyers and posters?"

Idea #2: "We charge $2.50 for each meal we deliver to the homebound seniors and handicapped people we serve. Yet, each meal costs the organization $5 to prepare and deliver. Let's increase the fees we charge for our Meals on Wheels program."

Piggyback on Idea #2: "I agree with your identification of the problem that the difference between what we charge and what it costs creates a deficit for our organization that we must address. I am concerned that increasing our fees for the meals we deliver will create a hardship for the economically disadvantaged people we serve. Could we consider approaching businesses through the Chamber of Commerce and Rotary Club to sponsor the program and provide them with recognition for their contribution? This could help us to make up the deficit in our program without burdening the people we serve."

Encourage Discussion

Often it appears that a few people dominate a discussion. Others stand back either because they are intimidated or they do not feel a part of the process. If they will be needed to become part of the solution, they should be involved in the discussion. Most people want to be heard. Often by probing and then layering your questions for more information you can encourage participation.

Examples:

1. Fund-raising problem: "John, you've had more experience with soliciting for large donations than anyone here. What do you think about offering multi-year gifts and the option to give appreciated assets as options when we speak with prospective donors?"

Layering: "What do you see as some of the benefits? What do we need to be careful about from your experience? Can we request a larger amount than we ordinarily might because we are asking for donations over a longer period? Are there any donors you have information on that would be helpful to us in finding the right people to ask for the gift?"

2. Volunteer recruitment problem: "Susan, you work closest with the volunteers. Do you have any ideas how we may increase the number of volunteers who would be attracted to work in our program?"

Layering: "What do you see as inhibiting factors for people who want to help, but do not step forward to volunteer? How important is the social aspect of the volunteers supporting and meeting each other to enhancing their experience? Should we be recruiting any particular types of people who make the best volunteers? If so, what are those characteristics most important to predicting high quality volunteers who will stay committed to the program?"

Use open-ended rather than closed-ended questions

Open-ended questions encourage discussion. Closed-ended questions can be answered either yes or no and tend to inhibit discussion. Have you noticed all the questions in the section on encouraging discussion were open-ended? Here are some closed-ended questions:

"John, should we offer multi-year gifts as an option for giving? Do you have the names of anyone we can ask to request the gift? Can you call and recruit them?"

"Susan, should we offer social events for our volunteers? Are we selective in the volunteers we recruit? Are we recruiting good enough people now?

Exercises

Choose a partner for a role-playing dyad. Each of you should prepare answers to provocative comments. Use the following statements and piggyback new ideas onto them.

- Women should not be paid as much as men for equivalent work because they usually do not provide sole support for a family.
- People convicted of a crime should receive mandatory prison sentences to discourage lawlessness.
  Illiterate people are stupid. Why waste the time trying to teach them to read when they are adults if they could not learn to read when they were kids like everyone else did.

Summary

Transactional communications, just like formal public speaking, can be learned with focused discipline and practice. The exercises provided in this chapter are only a starting point for the student to improve her/his skills. In the service sector, as in the private and public sectors, good informal and interactive communications skills are highly valued. In your community service volunteer work, try to observe how the best managers communicate and take every opportunity you can to practice your transactional communications skills in your internship experience.

CHAPTER 7

CALL TO SERVICE: SPEAKING AS A COMMUNITY LEADER

This paper explores the way leaders in the service and public sectors appeal to the sense of higher purpose to spur action to benefit society. Most of the activities the student intern or volunteer will experience in a service organization will be task oriented. So, most of the people you will encounter within the organization will be managing these projects. One of the advantages of volunteering or interning in a non-profit organization is that you can also be exposed or seek contact with the national, regional, and local leadership of the organization. There is a difference between leaders and managers. I have selected speech excerpts from national leadership in government, regional leadership in the service sector, and other prominent people in moral stature, so you can see how speaking as a community or national leader is a skill that can be studied, analyzed, and emulated by the speech communications student.

DISTINCTION BETWEEN LEADER AND MANAGER IN SERVICE ORGANIZATIONS

In their book, which is focused on the non-profit sector, "Leaders Who Make a Difference", Nanus and Dobbs (1999) state, "Leading and managing require two different mind and skill sets. Managers are chiefly responsible for processes and operations. They are mostly interested in what needs to be done and how it can be accomplished. In contrast, the leader is concerned with strategies and direction, with where the organization should be headed and what it can and should be doing in the future....Leaders prefer flexibility and change to predictability and control. They embrace complexity and uncertainty, because they know that change often provides new opportunities for service and may suggest innovative directions for future growth and development. Leaders are deemed successful when they enable their organizations to grow in their ability to serve the community, whether that be by discovering new community needs to satisfy, by expanding the resource base, or by energizing or transforming the organization itself."

Speaking as a Community Service Leader: Focus on Dr. Thomas Peters

A leader of a community service agency is often required to speak at a variety of public engagements. Dr. Thomas Peters is the Executive Director of the Marin Community Foundation, one of the largest community foundations in America. A community foundation provides financial support through grants to local organizations, ranging from the arts and education to human services and community development. A requirement for effectively speaking as a leader is the ability to adapt the concerns of the speaker and agency to the expectations and needs of a given audience and occasion. In the following excerpts of an address to an audience attending a conference on estate planning, Dr. Peters skillfully argues for the value of creating an enriching and lasting mark on one's community by creating a socially conscious legacy. This is a good example of a speaker selecting a topic of practical personal concern—estate planning—and linking it to a concept of higher social value.

Welcoming remarks delivered on October 23, 2002 at an estate planning seminar in Marin County, California.

On behalf of the Marin Community Foundation and the 45 nonprofit groups throughout the County who are co-sponsors of today's program, I want to extend a warm welcome to each of you. This is the eighth annual gathering in the County that we have collectively hosted to help you learn more about the complex and important subject of estate planning...I want to share some thoughts with you about the opportunities each of us has when we map out a strategy for planning our estates. Specifically, I want to talk about the notion of a legacy and how that can serve as a guide as you explore the important decisions you have chosen to make.

Legacy is one those words whose meaning has gradually expanded over time. Literally, it refers to tangible assets that are passed on from one generation to the next. So in that regard I assume that each of you is here today to learn more about how you can leave your own legacy to people and institutions most dear to you. But legacy has come to mean much more than one's tangible assets. It has come to embody a person's values—his or her reputation, passions, and interests—and the impact those resources have when they are passed on to future generations.

How a person's legacy is expressed and felt can vary greatly. It can be as grand as paving the way for powerful social change—when we speak, for example, of the legacy of Martin Luther King in fighting for the rights and dignity of all people.
It can be the support and encouragement of public institutions, as Andrew Carnegie did in the early part of the last century when he funded libraries in communities throughout our country. Or it could be as personal and private as a grandparent instilling in a grandchild a lifelong love of gardening or of Mozart.
Over the past couple of years the Foundation has explored the notion of legacy in still other ways. In trying to better understand the patterns and motivations for personal community involvement, we discovered that strong links between generations can promote greater awareness of, and involvement in, addressing community needs. We learned that young people who have been encouraged by their families to volunteer in the community are much more likely when they get older to contribute to local groups and continue their volunteer activities. This is an example of how the legacy of an entire generation can become the motivation people have to serve as the new stewards of their community...
In planning your estates, you are making a gift both of your financial resources and your values and passions. That is the real opportunity you have in making the kinds of decisions you are here to explore...What you give, and how you give it, can convey a lot about you, your wishes, and the impact you want to make. As an example, there has been quite a bit of discussion over the past several years about the impact of leaving large sums of money to children, and what that conveys to them about the value of working hard to achieve one's one benefits of success...this is an example of how a decision about your estate planning can also serve to convey to your children your values, and your wishes for their own relationship to money, to work, and to others.

In planning your estates, you also have the opportunity to leave a legacy for your community—to pass along your passion for the fine arts, your concern for the environment, or your appreciation for the education you received.

Think about any group or issue you have a special connection with, colleges, local food bank, literacy program, immigrant rights. Your interests are expressions of who you are. They help shape and express your values, your personalities, and your passions. By including them in your estate planning, you are ensuring that those who benefited from your generosity during your lifetime will continue to do so. And you will be passing the torch of caring to the next generation, helping to establish a family tradition of giving back.

Research indicates that relatively few Americans have considered charitable uses of their estates. In fact, if merely six percent of Americans left a charitable bequest—left a legacy to groups working on issues that matter most to them—the number of charitable bequests would more than double.

Leaving a legacy does not require having or leaving large amounts of money...People with more modest means have historically captivated our attention precisely because they left a considerable portion of their estate to a cause that touched their lives. Often their legacy reflected a generosity of spirit that was as powerful as one that involved huge fortunes.

I certainly do not want to leave you with the assumption that any of the decisions you are considering are easy ones. They each require us to acknowledge and confront nothing less than our own mortality...and to focus in very challenging ways on what really matters to us as individuals and as families.

As I look around this room, I also want to acknowledge that while you will be making decisions that are highly personal, you have chosen to consider them at a public event...a shared experience... In towns and cities across the country, nonprofit and other groups consider part of their mission to help people be as thoughtful and reflective as possible about how they will leave a legacy. It is our shared belief that this is a critical expression of belonging, of calling the place where you live your home... And that seeing what happens when individuals, families, and whole communities are given the chance and the support to flourish...what happens to someone when they have encouraging parents, inspirational teachers, a compassionate counselor or a safe neighborhood. These changes can literally last a lifetime. Your decisions about your estate planning—your legacy planning—can have the same kind of impact long after you and I are here.

Attending the event to learn methods to better preserve financial resources, the idea of establishing a legacy to enrich a community was not likely on the minds of many enrolled in this seminar. But Peters adapts his community-building agenda to an enlarged definition of estate planning to include using personal resources to promote the continuity of socially meaningful values. In this broader definition, Peters defines a community as one's extended heirs. He employs an interpersonal style that acknowledges the varied "highly personal" values and concerns of attendees, but also creates a collective sense of his audience as a community…"you have chosen to consider [decisions] at a public event…a shared experience. It is our shared belief that this is a critical expression of belonging."

In your study of persuasion you have likely examined Maslow's hierarchy of motivational needs and may recognize how this address fosters both our inherent need for group belonging and a higher sense personal esteem as incentives.

Peters also employs a deeply engrained cultural ethic, the "value of challenge" in describing the "impact of leaving large sums of money to children, and what that conveys to them about the value of working hard to achieve one's own benefits of success." This notion could resonate with an audience comprised of many self-made individuals.

Peters also presents rational evidence, pointing out that only six percent of Americans bequeath funds to agencies that "matter most to them" and that a simple doubling of such generosity would enormously enhance the outreach of service organizations. Yet, he also debunks the notion that legacies only involve the passing on of large fortunes, as the act "could be as personal and private as a grandparent instilling in a grandchild a lifelong love of gardening or of Mozart."

Incorporating a principle of behavior modification, a method that focuses on influencing behaviors as a precursor to attitude change, Peters points out that young people encouraged to engage in community service are more likely to continue such activities as adults.

Peters acknowledges that the subject of leaving a legacy carries emotional overtones of human mortality. Research finds that fear-provoking messages are most persuasive when the receiver is given incentives for the protection of loved ones and loved things. The tenor of much of Peters' speech focuses on the continuity of these most precious personal assets.

While Peters provides a strategically flexible definition of legacy, his audience likely consisted of some who met his ideas with initial resistance and others who found his appeal inspirational. A speaker facing varied levels of receptivity should consider whether a pragmatic or unifying style would best influence listeners. A pragmatic style suits listeners who may not share a speaker's position. For example, a proponent for preservation of a historical building addressing investors favoring a replacement high-rise with increased rental space, may pragmatically focus on concrete issues, rather than idealistic notions of paying homage to the past. The pragmatic speaker might stress that preserving the unique architectural character of an area would attract more patrons that would stimulate businesses.

A speaker addressing a sympathetic audience often finds a unifying style most effective. This approach can more freely use idealistic, artistic, narrative, and other consciousness-raising motivational appeals, as the audience's views are in concert with those of the speaker. An audience of preservationists would likely welcome an aesthetic appeal to restore the 1930's art deco glory of a theatre palace, accompanied with historical references honoring the age and the architect.

Peters blends both pragmatic and unifying styles in his address. His pragmatic dimension highlights tangible concepts like the monetary benefits of leaving a legacy. His unifying appeals stress altruism and investments that help preserve personal, family and community values.

ADVOCATING A NATIONAL SERVICE AGENDA

Peters challenges his audience to envision a legacy as both personally and socially rewarding. While Peters focuses on an individual's community consciousness, Presidents Kennedy and Clinton delivered noteworthy addresses requesting a national challenge, Kennedy in introducing ideas that germinated into the Peace Corp and Clinton in a signing ceremony initiating AmeriCorp. John Kennedy's impromptu speech delivered during the 1960 Presidential campaign appears below, along with excerpts of Bill Clinton's 1993 address.

Remarks delivered by Senator John F. Kennedy at the University of Michigan, October 14, 1960 (Kennedy campaigning as a candidate for President of the United States).

This speech was unrehearsed and delivered at 2:00 am while the candidate was on the campaign trail. The presence of the students surprised him and he honored their patience with the following impromptu speech. The speech represents Kennedy's first public statement of an idea that evolved into the Peace Corps. Although the key role of impromptu speaking is covered in the chapter on transactional communication, Kennedy's address is included here to demonstrate the need for social/political leaders to master the immediate qualities and demands of impromptu speaking.

I want to express my thanks to you, as a graduate of the Michigan of the East, Harvard University.

I come here tonight delighted to have the opportunity to say one or two words about this campaign that is coming into the last three weeks.

I think in many ways it is the most important campaign since 1933, mostly because of the problems which press upon the United States, and the opportunities which will be presented to us in the 1960's. The opportunity must be seized, through the judgment of the President, and the cooperation of the Congress. Through these I think we can make the greatest possible difference.

How many of you who are going to be doctors are willing to spend your days in Ghana? Technicians or engineers, how many of you are willing to work in the Foreign Service and spend your lives traveling around the world? On your willingness to do that, not merely to serve one year or two years in the service, but on your willingness to contribute part of your life to this country, I think will depend the answer whether a free society can compete.

Therefore, I am delighted to come to this University, because unless we have those resources in this school, unless you comprehend the nature of what is being asked of you, this country can't possibly move through the next ten years in a period of relative strength.

So I come here tonight to go to bed! But I also come here tonight to ask you to join in the effort... this University is not maintained by its alumni, or by the state, merely to help its graduates have an economic advantage. There is certainly a greater purpose, and I'm sure you recognize it. Therefore, I do not apologize for asking for your support in this campaign. I come here tonight asking your support for this country over the next decade.

John Kennedy's impromptu address resonates with the tenor of a campaign that summoned a spirit of citizen commitment to a higher cause. This speech anticipates his immortalized plea, "Ask not what your country can do for you. Ask for what you can do for your country." Like Thomas Peters, Kennedy appeals to the "Value of Challenge," a call that motivated many Americans in the height of the Cold War, when the Soviet Union had achieved spectacular series feats in its space program and had gained ideological influence in the Third World.

President William Jefferson Clinton: speech delivered at the Signing Ceremony of the National Community Service Trust Act inaugurating AmeriCorp, September 21, 1993.

When I went across this country last year, I was deeply moved by the forces that were both good and bad that kept pushing me to believe that this was more important than so many other things that all of us do in public life. I saw the wreckage, the insanity, the lost human potential that you can find in every community. And yet, I saw in the most difficult circumstances the light in the eyes of so many young people; the courage, the hunger to do something to reach beyond themselves and to reach out to others and to make things better.

I saw examples of the service programs represented on this stage. I watched the old and the young relate in ways they hadn't. I watched mean streets turn into safer, more humane places. I realized that there was no way any government program could solve these problems, but that the American people, if organized and directed and challenged, would find a way.

Twice before in this century Americans have been called to great adventures in civilian service. Sixty years ago, in the depths of the Depression, Franklin Roosevelt created the CCC and gave Americans the chance not only to do meaningful work so that they could feed themselves and their families, but so that they could build America for the future. There is not a state in this country that is untouched by the continuing impact of the work done by people who labored in the CCC.

It is with special pride that I will use President Roosevelt's pen set, with which he signed nearly every piece of legislation as President, to sign our bill today. We also point with pride to the enduring legacy and the continued vitality of John Kennedy's Peace Corps, created by legislation which President Kennedy signed 32 years ago tomorrow…

When I asked our country's young people to give something back to our country through grass-roots service, they responded by the thousands…I hope and believe that national service will remain throughout the life of

America not a series of promises, but a series of challenges, across all generations to help us to rebuild our troubled but wonderful land...

Beyond the concrete achievements of AmeriCorp, beyond the expanded educational opportunities those achievements will earn, national service will strengthen the cords that bind us as a people...

And I hope it will remind every American that there can be no opportunity without responsibility. The great English historian, Edward Given, warned that when the Athenians finally wanted not to give to society, but for society to give to them, when the freedom they wished for most was freedom from responsibility, then Athens ceased to be free...

This National Service Corps should send a loud and clear message across this country that the young people of America will preserve the freedom of America... by assuming the responsibility to rebuild the American family...

I ask you only to remember that as we move toward the 21st century, the success our great voyage, the longest experiment in free society in human history—to remember that it is at the grass roots that we will succeed or fail. Today we take a stand for the proposition that if we challenge people to serve and we give them a chance to fulfill their abilities, we will understand that we must go forward together. And it will be the great legacy of the wonderful people who make it come alive.

The Kennedy and Clinton speeches illustrate the importance of linking historical service programs to new endeavors, as they associate the forging of a program with a rich and revered tradition. The CCC (Civilian Conservation Corp) assumes nearly mythical status in their rhetoric, with the suggestion that proposed endeavors and programs can yield similar spirits and results. The "Value of Challenge" is again a constant thread in these calls to service. In a time of diminishing government services and increasing public need, summoning citizens to help provide solutions assumes the status and emotion of heroic action, a compelling unifying appeal.

Activity
Kennedy and Clinton both employ a unifying style appropriate for enthusiastic supporters. Kennedy addressed college students willing to wait until 2:00 AM to glimpse the charismatic candidate. Clinton spoke before an audience that helped conceive AmeriCorp.

Using a pragmatic strategy focusing on practical audience benefits which typically rely less on emotional appeals and more on rationale and concrete argument, how could a community leader motivate a group of college students worried about careers in a weak job market to engage in volunteer service? Before beginning your discussion in small groups, first agree upon the following:

- Specifically define the composition of the audience, the setting, and the speaker.
- Determine if the speaker would offer a menu of volunteer choices, or one specific opportunity.
- Discuss what pragmatic incentives would be provided.
- Would any unifying incentives be effective?
- Is there an appeal to a higher social value that would help persuade this group?
- What persuasive concepts studied in class would bolster the message?
- What specific action-step would the speaker request?

Honoring the Achievements and Maturation of AmeriCorp

AmeriCorp Graduation Address delivered by Leslie Lenkowsky, CEO for the Corporation for National Community Service, July 22, 2003

While President Clinton helped to establish AmeriCorp in the early 1990's, it is interesting to move the calendar forward to 2003 to determine how a social leader developed a ceremonial speech to acknowledge the maturity, accomplishments, and historical place of this organization. In July, 2003 Leslie Lenkowsky, CEO of the Corporation for National and Community Service, delivered a commencement address for graduates of AmeriCorp: National Civilian Community Corp (NCCC), a program requiring a 10-month residential training for men and women between ages 18-24. The speech took place at the NCCC campus in Charleston South Carolina. In the following excerpts from Lenkowsky's address, examine how he employs three principles of effective speech to link the accomplishments of the organization to the traditions and future of public service: personalized narrative to create immediacy with the audience; time-binding—connecting AmeriCorp with a historically significant national service program;

metaphor, a strategic comparison of two dissimilar concepts. This speech illustrates how metaphors of unity are often common in times of social crisis.

1. The speaker employs a narrative opening to personalize the address and to preview the time-honored lineage of the NCCC. The evocative introduction encourages audience participation through visualization of a storyline.

A few months ago, my wife, Kate, and I attended a conference in Amelia Island, Florida. During our free time one morning, we took a stroll through a beautiful, if gator-inhabited state park, overlooking Cumberland Sound and Jacksonville Harbor. We had been told that there was a well-restored, Civil War-era coastal fort in the park, just like the fort shown at the end of the movie "Glory." After an hour or so of hiking, we came upon Fort Clinch and it was just as advertised, including the "re-enactors" in costume to tell visitors about how the fort operated. However, what really got my attention—and made me feel very proud—was a sign at the entrance to the fort. It said that the fort had been restored in the 1930's by the Civilian Conservation Corp [CCC].

2. Creating linkage and continuity with historical and contemporary symbols, events, and organizations is called "time-binding." This device is especially effective when a current subject is associated with a revered subject from the past. In the following excerpts Lenkowsky describes AmeriCorp: NCCC as emerging from the spirit and purpose of the Civilian Conservation Corp., a government program that put hundreds of thousands of Americans to work and helped to restore public hope during the Great Depression (again, note the common thread with the Kennedy and Clinton addresses).

Most of you know that the original CCC, begun in 1933 by President Franklin Delano Roosevelt shortly after his inauguration, was the inspiration behind the program from which you are graduating today. At that time, America was struggling to recover from a terrible economic setback—the Great Depression. Millions upon millions of Americans had been thrown out of work. Families everywhere were extremely apprehensive about losing all that they had worked so hard to build...

To many of those who served, the CCC was perhaps the most formative and transformative experience in their lives. What's more, many former members of the CCC feel a special bond with AmeriCorp: NCCC and—though their numbers are dwindling—continue to appear regularly at NCCC inductions and graduations. Their involvement serves as living reminder that every one of you is part of a great tradition of service in this nation…You have created a link for yourselves with the millions upon millions of Americans, past and present, who have felt a debt of gratitude for their freedoms and expressed that debt through service. In short, just as the members of the CCC did, you have become part of American history, leaving a mark that will benefit our country for many years to come.

3. Assessing the effects of September 11 on the American psyche and the need for the nation to respond with increased civic participation, Lenkowsky uses metaphor to establish service as a moral imperative, in fact, the 'moral equivalent of war.'

At the beginning of the 20th century, a Harvard professor, William James, talked about national service as being 'the moral equivalent of war.' He was engaged in the great issues of his time, especially—in pre World War I days—whether or not mankind might avoid the scourge of war. However, James recognized that if worldwide peace ever did break out, there might be a problem: how could nations constructively channel the aggressive energies of those who fought in the military? 'Civilian service,' he believed, was the answer, and it received practical expression when on of his former students became President and created the CCC…

Can national service play a useful role in furnishing the equivalent of war without the great and terrible costs of combat? Especially in an era of a high-tech, low manpower military, can it provide an effective way of enabling more Americans to express concretely their feeling of gratitude for the blessing of liberty they enjoy? And can the ability of national service programs to engage Americans who only have a few hours each week or month to volunteer be a tool for maintaining and increasing civic spirit and engagement, long after al-Qaeda, Saddam Hussein, and our other adversaries are vanquished?

In my first official speech as CEO of the Corporation, in October 2001, I told a group of NCCC inductees in Washington that they had the opportunity to give historians of the future real cause to debate which generation was, indeed, the greatest. Those of you graduating today truly are the Nine-One-One Generation, the first to come to adulthood in the post—September 11 world, a world that is more precarious, more uncertain, more challenging than the world inherited by those who came before you.

Activity

Working individually or in a group, determine how a contemporary social service campaign could profit from using a time-bound historical symbol, movement, and/or figure to enhance a specific persuasive appeal (e.g., an environmental group invoking the name of John Muir or posting the luminous white and blue image of our planet taken by Apollo astronauts to promote participation in Earth Day). Assess your audience to determine what time-bound subjects would best complement your central purpose and resonate with message recipients. Your message could be composed for a flyer, a one-minute public service announcement for radio or television, a poster with an image and caption, etc.

The Bridge from Ethos to Pathos and Logos: Classic Tools for Leadership

A Whisper of AIDS: Address to the 1992 Republican National Convention in Houston by Mary Fisher.

Effective leadership is often dependent on the confluence of personality meeting conditions. While studying the history of U.S. international relations, you may have come across the claim, "Only Nixon could have gone to China." This statement refers to President Nixon's restoration of diplomatic relations with China in the early 1970's. The United States had severed diplomatic ties with China after that country had instituted a communist government.

Nixon came to political prominence as an anti-communist in the late 1940's and early 50's. His anti-communist credentials provided the credibility for his reestablishing relations with China. A president pursuing the same diplomatic policy during the Cold War, but lacking Nixon's credentials, may have been viewed as negotiating with an adversary from a position of weakness.

The successful confluence of character and condition, or more specifically, that of speaker and occasion and audience, occurred when Mary Fisher delivered her "A Whisper of AIDS" speech to the 1992 National Republican Convention. At the time, the Republican Party was criticized by many as insensitive to the spreading AIDS epidemic. Some elements in the party passed it off as a "gay illness."

Twenty thousand delegates filled the Astrodome for Fisher's speech. Fisher, HIV positive, was a young mother from an affluent background, heterosexual, a graduate of elite schools, and with an impressive Republic pedigree (having worked in President Ford's administration). Her postcard image and background could hardly provoke defensive reactions from her audience. She became the ideal person to deliver a plea that her party open its heart and come to better understand the complexity and severity of the AIDS epidemic.

After reading her address, let's explore Aristotle's classic framework to determine how her ethos (perceived credibility and character) helped magnify the power of her emotional (pathos) and logical (logos) appeals.

A Whisper of AIDS

Less than three months ago, at platform hearings in Salt Lake City, I asked the Republican Party to lift the shroud of silence which has been draped over the issue of HIV/AIDS. I have come tonight to bring our silence to an end.

I bear a message of challenge, not self-congratulation. I want your attention, not your applause. I would never have asked to be HIV-positive. But I believe that in all things there is a good purpose, and so I stand before you and before the nation, gladly.

The reality of AIDS is brutally clear. Two hundred thousand Americans are dead or dying; a million more are infected. Worldwide forty million, or sixty million or a hundred million infections will be counted in the coming years. But despite science and research, White House meetings and congressional hearings, despite good intentions and bold initiatives, campaign slogans and hopeful promises—despite it all, it's the epidemic which is winning tonight.

In the context of an election year, I ask you—here, in this great hall, or listening in the quiet of your home—to recognize that the AIDS virus is not an apolitical creature. It does not care whether you are black or white, male or female, gay or straight, young or old.

Tonight, I represent an AIDS community whose members have been reluctantly drafted from every segment of American society. Though I am white and a mother, I am one with a black infant struggling with tubes in a Philadelphia hospital. Though I am female and contracted this disease in marriage, and enjoy the warm support of my family, I am one with the lonely gay man sheltering a flickering candle from the cold wind of his family's rejection.

Infection is increasing fastest among women and children. Largely unknown a decade ago, AIDS is the third leading killer of young-adult Americans today—but it won't be third for long. Because, unlike other diseases, this one travels. Adolescents don't give each other cancer or heart disease because they believe they are in love. But HIV is different, and we have helped it along. We have killed each other—with our ignorance, our prejudice, and our silence.

We may take refuge in our stereotypes but cannot hide there long. Because HIV asks only one thing of those it attacks: Are you human? People with HIV have not entered some alien state of being. They are human. They have not earned cruelty and they do not deserve meanness. They don't benefit from being isolated or treated as outcasts. Each of them is exactly what God made: a person. Not evil, deserving of our judgment; not victims, longing for our pity. People. Ready for support and worthy of compassion...

My call to the nation is a plea for awareness. If you believe you are safe, you are in danger. Because I was not hemophiliac, I was not at risk. Because I was not gay, I was not at risk. Because I did not inject drugs, I was not at risk.

My father has devoted much of his lifetime to guarding against another holocaust. He is part of the generation that heard Pastor Neimoeller come out of the Nazi death camps to say, 'They came after the Jews and I was not a Jew, so I did not protest. They came after the Trade Unionists, and I was not a Trade Unionist, so I did not protest. They came after the Roman Catholics, and I was not a Roman Catholic. Then they came after me, and there was no one left to protest.'

127

The lesson history teaches is this: If you believe you are safe, you are at risk. If you do not see this killer stalking your children, look again. There is no family or community, no race or religion, no place left in America that is safe. Until we genuinely embrace this message, we are a nation at risk.

Tonight, HIV marches resolutely towards AIDS in more than a million American homes, littering its pathway with the bodies of the young. Young men. Young women. Young parents. Young Children. One of the families is mine. If it is true that HIV inevitably turns to AIDS, then my children will inevitably turn to orphans.

My family has been a rock of support. My 84-year-old father, who has pursued the healing of nations, will not accept the premise that he cannot heal his daughter. My mother has refused to be broken; she still calls at midnight to tell wonderful jokes that make me laugh. Sisters and friends, and my brother Phillip all have helped carry me over the hardest places. I am blessed, richly and deeply blessed, to have such a family.

But not all of you have been so blessed. You are HIV-positive but dare not say it. You have lost loved ones, but you dared not whisper the word AIDS. You weep silently; you grieve alone.

I have a message for you: It is not you who should feel shame, it is we. We who tolerate ignorance and practice prejudice, we who have taught you to fear. We must lift our shroud of silence, making it safe for you to reach out for compassion. It is our task to seek safety for our children, not in quiet denial but in effective action.

Some day our children will be grown. My son Max, now four, will take the measure of his mother; my son Zachary, now two, will sort through his memories. I may not be here to hear their judgments, but I know already what I hope they are.

I want my children to know that their mother was not a victim. She was a messenger. I do not want them to think, as I once did, that courage is the absence of fear; I want them to know that courage is the strength to act wisely when we are most afraid. I want them to have the courage to step forward when called by their nation, or their party, and give leadership—no matter what the personal cost. I ask no more of you than I ask of myself, or of my children.

To the millions of you who are grieving, who are frightened, who have suffered the ravages of AIDS firsthand: Have courage and you will find comfort.

To the millions who are strong, I issue this plea: Set aside prejudice. To my children, I make this pledge: I will not give in, Zachary, because I draw my courage from you. Your silly giggle gives me hope. Your gentle prayers give me strength. And you, my child, give me reason to say to America, "You are at risk." And I will not rest, Max, until I have done all I can to make your world safe. I will seek a place where intimacy is not the prelude to suffering.

I will not hurry to leave you, my children. But when I go, I pray that you will not suffer shame on my account.

To all within sound of my voice, I appeal: Learn with me the lessons of history and of grace, so my children will not be afraid to say the word AIDS when I am gone. Then their children, and yours, may not need to whisper it at all.

God bless the children, and bless us all.

In practical application, the potential effectiveness of pathos relates to the emotional receptivity of an audience. The effects of emotional appeals, however, do not act independently. Ethos, the perceived credibility and charisma of a communicator, influences the effectiveness of emotional appeals. For example, audiences typically react negatively to emotionally charged fear appeals delivered by a speaker viewed as possessing low credibility. In such cases, emotional appeals are often perceived as manipulative ploys that serve the advantage of the speaker.

In attempting to identify the elements of ethos, three central components emerge, trustworthiness, expertise, and sincerity. Audiences tend to believe people who convey trustworthiness and sincerity. Delegates at the 1992 Republican Convention quite naturally identified with Mary Fisher's image. In appearance, background, and service experience, she was one of them. Fisher's HIV condition gave her firsthand knowledge of the pain and stigma of the illness. The audience's ability to extend sympathy, rather than defensive reaction, was largely a result of Fisher's perceived ethos.

Dynamic persuasion may also emanate from quiet, but powerful tones that convey thoughtful and deeply felt emotions. Fisher's solemn delivery crossed into the realm of moving pathos, especially in combination with a text that evoked personal courage and identity with an unpopular position.

Fisher's message exhibited other Aristotelian characteristics of pathos, namely justice, generosity, and magnanimity, as expressed through her personal identification with the rights and needs of every AIDS victim and her call for society to extend comfort and care to all. Throughout her address, we see a joining of ethos and pathos.

Exercise

It is simplistic to view Aristotle's artistic proofs of ethos, pathos, and logos as independent elements of persuasion. Mary Fisher's address also contains fact-based qualities of logos. Review her text, singling out logos-based proofs. For class-wide discussion be prepared to assess how Fisher's projection of ethos and pathos may have influenced the impact of her rational data. How might a speech with more emphasis on logos and less reliance on ethos and pathos have been received?

GUIDELINES TO INTRODUCE A FEATURED SPEAKER

The service sector provides the student with opportunities to learn how to introduce featured speakers for formal events, as well as introduce individuals to each other. While we all have introduced and been introduced many times in our lives, the occasion for formal introductions provides the chance to use our speech communications skills to enhance and "set the stage" in a dramatic way. Indeed, the non-profit service sector may be the most fertile ground to provide inspiring introductions, because the speaker will be related to a *cause or endeavor with higher social value.*

The overall goal of the speech to introduce is to both establish what the higher value is for the cause and the relationship and impact this individual has on advancing the cause.

The tasks in a speech to introduce may consist of several parts:

1. Thank and honor those who are present and provide the context for why they are in attendance. Describe the cause of the organization, and how attendees are connected to the cause.
2. Identify the societal need that is being addressed. Present the cause as important, noble, urgent, uplifting, and any other relevant way to enhance the organization or cause. Use specific information and

evidence to support your premise that the need is great. Appropriately thank those in the audience for their efforts and partnership in moving the cause ahead.

3. Introduce the person by providing their background, accomplishments, awards, titles, and any other relevant personal information to show their dedication to the cause or organization and the importance of their efforts to the cause.

Case study

America's Promise is a national service organization that recruits, trains, and assigns volunteer tutors to work with disadvantaged youth to improve reading skills. The organization seeks time and talent from volunteers and funding from corporations and foundations to accomplish its mission.

The occasion is Washington State Governor Gary Locke's remarks to introduce America's Promise Chairman Retired General Colin Powell. The State of Washington is creating the Washington Reading Corps, designed to give teachers and principals the resources of volunteers and donated funds to mobilize local communities to improve the reading scores of early grade children. Here are excerpts from the speech that illustrate the principle tasks for the speech to introduce.

1. Thank and honor those who are present and provide the context for their attendance. Describe the cause of the organization, and how attendees are connected to the cause.

"Today I am extremely proud to see so many of Washington's business and community leaders and citizens stepping forward and making commitments to our children. You are the heart of America's Promise.

Washington's Promise is a statewide effort to inspire Washingtonians of all backgrounds and from the business, non-profit, faith communities and government to reach the goals of the Presidents' Summit for America's Future. (The Presidents' Summit for America's Future had been established a year prior to this presentation)

The response to the Presidents' summit in our state, "Washington's Promise" is a host of new initiatives and contributions of time, talent, and funds all coordinated to complement and stimulate existing efforts to help our youth.

The effort calls on all of us to roll up our sleeves and make the time to help our children be successful."

2. Identify the societal need that is being addressed. Present the cause as important, noble, urgent, uplifting, and any other relevant way to enhance the organization or cause. Use specific information and evidence to support your premise that the need is great. Appropriately thank the audience for their efforts and interest in partnership toward moving the cause ahead.

"Unfortunately, we know some children are falling through the cracks. Last fall we received our first test results that tell us how well our fourth graders are measuring up to our new academic standards.

Less than half of our fourth graders met our standard in reading. Now these kids are in the fifth grade. It is not enough to tell their parents that our schools will do better with next year's first and second graders. Last year's fourth graders need help now and so do this year's first, second, third, and fourth-graders.

That's why the first and most important partnership I'm calling for is the creation of the Washington Reading Corps.

Instead of just giving schools money and telling them to fix the problem, the Reading Corps is designed to give teachers and principals the resources they need to mobilize their entire communities.

The goal of this program is to recruit 25,000 volunteers all across the state. Teachers trained in the most effective methods of teaching reading would then supervise and work with the tutors to help 82,000 children in reading...

You and I know that tutoring works and that children need individualized attention. And we know that if children fall in the early grades it is unlikely they will ever catch up. That is why the commitments you've made to Washington's children today are so important. Your volunteer efforts working with our children do make a difference. Your volunteerism is how a lifetime of success gets started and how a lifetime of frustration and failure is averted.
So I want to thank you for helping Washington get started on the road to success and keep our promise."

3. Introduce the person by providing their background, accomplishments, awards, titles, and any other relevant personal information to show how dedicated they are to the cause or organization and how important their efforts have been for the cause.

"And we can all be inspired to keep the promise of helping our children succeed by the dedication and leadership of General Powell. In less than one year, General Powell has led America's promise from a great idea to a national movement. He has inspired our nation to return to the value of service to others and called out to all Americans to be better citizens.

He has harnessed the energy and power of countless communities, business, labor organizations, service organizations, and people of all walks of life and all ages. More importantly, he has drawn our focus to both the needs and promise of America's youth.

Our state is indeed fortunate to be inspired to even greater levels of commitment to our children by General Powell's appearance at today's summit. And I'm deeply honored to be able to introduce Retired General Colin Powell, Chairman of America's Promise---The Alliance for Youth.

General Powell is the winner of two presidential medals of freedom and numerous military awards. He is a member of the Board of Trustees of Howard University and a member of the Board of Director of the United Negro College Fund. General Powell also serves on the Board of Governors of the Boys and Girls Clubs of America, and is an advisory member of the Children's Health Fund.

So please join me in welcoming one of the great leaders of our time, General Colin Powell.

Exercise

Use these five task guidelines to create an introduction of someone who is the president or executive director of a non-profit organization you are involved with. Or as an example for your exercise you may choose to introduce the Executive Director of the United Way in your community. Imagine you are introducing the Executive Director, who will thank the volunteer leadership gathered for the successful conclusion of the United Way campaign for the year. You can research the United Way in your community by calling their office and by searching on their website at http://national.unitedway.org/myuw/ e

Here is a checklist to follow as you construct your speech to introduce:

1. What is the purpose of the organization? Can it be summarized in one sentence?

Sample
"Washington's Promise is a statewide effort to inspire Washingtonians of all backgrounds and from business, non-profit, faith communities and government to reach the goals of the President's Summit for America's Future."

2. Who is the audience and what is their connection to the organization?

Sample:
"Washington's business and community leaders and citizens stepping forward and making commitments to our children"

3. What is the societal need and how is it being addressed?

Sample:
"Unfortunately, we know some children are falling though the cracks...Less than half our fourth graders met our standard in reading.

The goal of the program is to recruit 25,000 volunteers all across the state. Teachers trained in the most effective methods of teaching would then supervise and work with the tutors to help 82,000 children in reading.

4. What is the connection of the person introduced to the cause? What can be said to show how this person emulates the values of the organization? What relevant information should be used to establish their credibility to the audience?

Sample:
"Retired General Colin Powell, Chairman of America's Promise---The Alliance for Youth...He has led America's promise from a great idea to a national movement. He has inspired our nation to return to the value of service to others and called out to all Americans to be better citizens"

5. List awards and honors for this individual.

Sample:
General Powell is the winner of two presidential medals of freedom and numerous military awards. He is a member of the Board of Trustees of Howard University and a member of the Board of Director of the United Negro College Fund. General Powell also serves on the Board of Governors of the Boys and Girls Clubs of America, and is an advisory member of the Children's Health Fund.

PRESENTING A VISION FOR PUBLIC POLICY

Colin Powell, former chairman of the Joint Chiefs of Staff and Secretary of State under the Bush Administration, has often served as a proponent of the values and actions to include the poor and dispossessed in the enactment of public policy and the engagement of the private sector in making America a better place for all.

In Colin Powell's address to the Republican Convention in 2000, the excerpts below illustrate his mastery of public speaking techniques through his appeal to fairness in policy to those who are disadvantaged. It is particularly noteworthy that this message of inclusion and the call for fighting discrimination, which appeals to core values of the Democratic Party, is not usually emphasized in the Republican Party. Notice how Colin Powell through communication of shared values links this message to a Republican audience.

"The Republican Party must always be the party of inclusion. The Hispanic immigrant that became a citizen yesterday must be as precious to us as a Mayflower descendent. The descendent of a slave or struggling miner in Appalachia must be as welcome and must find as much appeal in our party as in any other party or in any other American life. It is our diversity that has made us strong. Yet our diversity throughout our American history has also been a source of discrimination which we as guardians of the American dream must rip out branch and root."

Analysis
Powell links the status of the people who relate to their origins to early Mayflower immigrants as a precious privilege to the principle of diversity and appreciation of a wide variety of backgrounds, including the dispossessed, as an American strength. In essence, he uses this appreciation

for diversity as a rationale for fighting discrimination, so we can guard the American Dream. This line of reasoning links inclusion, appreciation of all diversity as an American strength, to the action of fighting discrimination as a core American value.

Exercises

1. Why do you think Powell chose the recent Hispanic immigrant that became a citizen yesterday, the descendent of a slave, and the struggling miner in Appalachia as the examples for the principle of inclusion? Why is this an important point to make to a Republican Party Convention?

2. How does Powell link diversity to discrimination? How does he link the fight against discrimination as a patriotic act? What does the phrase "guardians of the American dream" mean to the audience and why does this phrase have significance for the audience?

In another excerpt from the same speech, we can see how Powell links his message to a shared value in the recognition of Abraham Lincoln as an exemplar of the Republican Party. It is the values of Lincoln that validate Powell's claim that these are indeed core Republican values.

"It is our party, the party of Lincoln, that must always stand with equal rights and fair opportunity for all. And where discrimination still exists, where the scars of past discrimination still contaminate and disfigure the present, let us not close our eyes to it and declare there is a level playing field and hope that it will go away by itself. It did not in the past. It will not in the future. Let the party of Lincoln be in the forefront, leading the crusade, not only to cut off and kill discrimination, but to open every avenue of educational and economic opportunity to those who are still denied access because of their race, ethnic background or gender."

Analysis

Powell is providing this perspective because he believes it is important for the Republican Party to stand for these principles and capture the loyalty and votes of African Americans, immigrants, economically disadvantaged people, and those who seek societal redress from the federal government in laws and policies. These opinions, therefore, are expressed with the purpose to build a larger base for the Republican Party.

In this chapter we can see that speaking effectively as a leader in the service and public policy sectors demands command of speech communication practices. In the speeches provided, you can see a variety of styles and topics that show how leadership inspires service for the public good by affecting attitudes and motivating people through the value of challenge to dedicate themselves to the improvement of society.

References

Nanus, Burt, Dobbs, Stephen M. (1999) Leaders Who Make a Difference: Essential Strategies for Meeting the Non-profit Challenge, (1st ed.). San Francisco: Jossey-Bass

CHAPTER 8

DESIGNING MEDIA MESSAGES FOR A CALL TO COMMUNITY SERVICE: TECHNIQUES FROM THE ADVERTISING WORLD.

This paper introduces principles and methods for message analysis for media delivered communications for the service sector. Through the selected examples of varied media communications, the student can better understand the rhetorical underpinnings of media delivered messages and how these methods can be adapted to improve speech communications.

By the time Americans have reached 18, they have already seen thousands of hours of movies, TV, and commercials. So it is fair to say that the average college student has developed a fine sense of visual sophistication for the rhetoric of media delivered messages that combine sight, sound and motion. In addition, we carry this rhetorical discernment of media messaging to outdoor billboards, magazine ads, radio commercials, and internet delivered banner ads.

In mid-twentieth century, Marshall McLuhan (1964) was a visionary who foresaw the coming dramatic changes in how media technologies would connect everyone on earth in what he termed a "Global Village". His prophetic vision predated, yet correctly anticipated, the global satellite and internet technology that has enabled worldwide connectivity. He proposed that the ubiquity of media in our lives changes our experience of messages and each other. In a concise and provocative statement of this concept, he coined the phrase "The Medium is the Message". McLuhan believed that our experience of the media itself, regardless of message content, alters our perceptions of events, people, and how we view reality. He states: "The effects of technology do not occur at the levels of opinions or concepts, but alter sense ratios or patterns of perceptions steadily and without any resistance."

Since so much of our thinking, opinions and perceptions of how we experience the world is affected by media delivered messages, it is appropriate to examine some of the rhetorical approaches in public service advertising and graphics that are adopted from communications techniques developed for commercial products.

Despite conventional wisdom that the image-makers of advertising can control and brainwash the masses, the hard truth is that advertising in a free marketplace does not have the power to control thinking and action. When successful, commercial advertising can help to create an identity for a brand, positive feelings about a company or entity, or preference for a product. In the service-learning arena we will examine how the same techniques to sell products can be used to influence public policy and charitable inclination. The use of media can also increase our interest in a cause, communicate benefits of the cause, and persuade people to gain additional information or take action for the cause.

Here is a definition of advertising in the service sector and its links to student public speech/communication:

Advertising is intended to create awareness and preference for a particular cause so that the message recipient understands, agrees with, and takes a recommended action for the advertised cause.

The Appeal to Values

Advertisers build campaigns based on shared values just as speakers do when they address an audience.

Some people may object that this comparison of value is pure nonsense. Aren't we manipulating unsuspecting people to perceive needs they do not have by using the media to induce them to opinions and actions encouraged by the tricks of media editing and entertainment? Of course, the same can be said for the rhetorical techniques of good speakers and their influence on the audiences.

The point is to be successful, value must be understood, and is sometimes difficult to determine. As the humorous quote below illustrates, what constitutes "real value" depends on individual point of view.

> "The Cynic is one who knows the price of everything and the value of nothing".
> ---*Oscar Wilde*, 19th century English playwright

People perceive value in many ways. They can perceive value both in terms of logic of an argument *or* through satisfaction of an *emotional need*. How I feel about the cause or problem portrayed will determine how ready I am to be positively inclined to take action to support that cause.

The Civil Society and the Political Process: Public Communication for Public Policy

To understand the dynamics of the non-profit service sector and its role in society, it is important to recognize this sector as connected to the economic (private) and the government (public) sectors. The non-profit sector plays a vital role in the dynamic of a free society through its interaction with the other two.

Michael Mandelbaum (2002), points out that civil non-profit organizations are part of a civil society. They are in a dynamic relationship with the economic private and government societies.

"But politics and economics are more than closely connected. They overlap in a crucial way. A market economy is the basis for one of the main features of modern liberal political systems---civil society. Civil society consists of the independent social organizations---religious and professional groups, labor unions, civic organizations---that stand between the society's basic unit, the family, and the state. Civil society contributes to both parts of liberal politics. It gives weight to constitutional restrictions by providing a counterbalancing force to the state. A private economic sector is a base from which to criticize and oppose what the government does. And it is the locus of much of the political activity associated with popular sovereignty. In the core democracies electoral competition takes place between and among political parties, important institutions of civil society. Parties are organized to represent interests and the most important ones they represent are economic ones."

It is with this understanding of the complex and dynamic relationship of the sectors of the society that we can appreciate the context for an analysis of the non-profit media campaign "We Want Change." This was a communications campaign in 2003, funded by a coalition of San Francisco businesses and non-profit organizations to address the issue of pandemic panhandling on the streets, while large sums of tax dollars designated for care of the homeless were not being spent properly. By understanding how media communication techniques are employed in persuasion, students can become more effective public speakers and social advocates.

THE RHETORICAL ANALYSIS OF THE SERVICE CAMPAIGN "WE WANT CHANGE"

One of the most difficult issues we face in advertising is how to critique an advertising idea. Within the advertising industry there are many theories and approaches to development of advertising ideas, just as in public speaking/communication. These are two approaches to developing advertising to help you better understand the "We Want Change" campaign: Unique Selling Proposition and Juxtaposition of Known Elements in a New Way.

Unique Selling Proposition

Unique Selling Proposition Definition: *Focus upon the selling idea and create a memorable execution that links the advertising execution to the unique position of the product in the consumer's mind.*

Unique Selling Proposition (USP) was first articulated by Rosser Reeves (1961).

Some of the most well known advertising campaigns were developed using this simple approach to advertising development. Here are some examples:

- M&M's: Melt in Your Mouth, Not in Your Hands.

- Wisk: Ring Around the collar

- Wonderbread: Helps Build Bodies Twelve Ways

- Certs: Two Mints in One

The USP is a powerful tool to help create an identity for the product or idea based on a memorable device to symbolize it in a way that is meaningful, important and believable to the target audience. The advertiser can create a distinction for the idea based on the consumer remembering the identity or message through the jingle or key visual of the advertising execution.

The principle of USP can be effectively used in speech communications to help identify a concept (either positively or negatively) as this example shows.

During the Reagan administration (1980-88), there was a U.S. Senate debate over the proposed major funding for a program to develop a high tech missile shield to defend the U.S. against the launch of a nuclear missile by the Soviet Union, a rogue state, or a terrorist group. In arguing against the funding of this program as wasteful and not likely to succeed, Senator Edward Kennedy used the phrase "Star Wars". This was a way to denigrate the program by comparing it to the popular movie "Star Wars", which was a fictional and fanciful account of high-tech warfare. The term "Star Wars" then stuck in popular reference to describe this program.

Exercise: See if you can identify some of your favorite ads through their use of a jingle or key visual: Here are some examples:

Jingles or Headlines

Got milk? (Milk Advisory Board)
The Best a Man Can Get (Gilette)
This Bud's For You (Budweiser Beer)

Visuals
Swish line (Nike)
Double Yellow Arches (McDonalds)
Stage Coach (Wells Fargo Bank)

Exercise

Can you identify jingles, headlines, or visuals in social service advertising campaigns in your community? If so, explain how these communications devices help people to better understand and remember the message?

Juxtaposition of known elements in a new way

Consider this distinction about credibility. We can use unbelievable executions in advertising to gain interest and make a point. What is important is that the claim being made is credible, not the advertising execution itself.

We will illustrate this approach in the example of "We Want Change Ad". Even though we know that the people pictured who are well dressed and prosperous would not hold up a cardboard sign, we understand that the communications idea of "We Want Change" is to break through the conventional portrayal of the logical arguments and facts with a visual (a cardboard sign that homeless people frequently hold when they panhandle) that is unusual and yet relevant to the message of the campaign: Panhandling is a blight on the community and does not help address the problems of homeless people.

Combining familiar elements in combinations we are not used to seeing creates interest, because it is fresh and original. This principle works very well to illustrate a USP, because viewers usually pay more attention to communications that intrigues them. In the case of the "We want Change Campaign" the USP is the well dressed person holding up a cardboard sign of the type frequently used by homeless people, but with the message that the city of San Francisco is not using the resources to help the homeless and thereby reduce panhandling. We remember the campaign idea: the city should address its resources for the homeless. The images of well-dressed citizens and business people holding these signs are intended to affect public policy towards homelessness and panhandling.

This communications campaign, developed in the civil sector, actually did have an impact on the public sector. It coalesced political support around Gavin Newsom for Mayor of San Francisco, who ran a on a platform incorporating the theme "Care not Change". Newsom won the election in November 2003.

So, if we use simple criteria to evaluate this campaign, here are some questions we can ask:

Is there an advertising idea? Absolutely. The citizens of San Francisco want to see a stop to street panhandling. The city government is responsible to improve its use of the large resources spent on homeless people to solve this problem. The juxtaposition of the elements of the cardboard sign, the well dressed citizen, and the message for change in public policy written on the sign are all known elements combined in a new way to bring inherent drama and interest to the message.

Is the idea clear? As clear as a bell! Panhandling is a hassle for everyone and the city should reduce and eliminate it.

Is it simple? The statement handwritten on the cardboard sign combined with the status of the people holding the sign are easily and immediately understood.

Does the headline and visual communicate the message? The message on the sign is the headline and the cardboard sign and the individual demonstrating in San Francisco is the visual medium. They work synergistically to deliver a powerful, persuasive message.

Exercise

Just as in the "We Want Change" campaign, often public policy is influenced by grass-roots civil society efforts to change or enforce laws to address societal problems. One such example is MADD (Mothers Against Drunk Driving).

As a group exercise, develop the ideas for print ads directed to college students on behalf of MADD using the advertising techniques of unique selling proposition and juxtaposition of known elements in a new way.

Here are some questions to help your group develop your advertising campaign and facts to work with excerpted from the MADD website (www.MADD.org):

1- What does MADD do, why is its work important, and why is its focus now on preventing underage drinking?

"MADD's mission is to stop drunk driving, support the victims of this violent crime and prevent underage drinking. We have formally embraced the prevention of underage drinking because of the extent of this terrible problem and its impact on drunk driving.

Alcohol is the No. 1 drug problem facing our nation's youth-killing 6.5 times more young people than all other illicit drugs combined. In the next five to 10 years, the U.S. will see a large influx of new drivers, as children of

Baby Boom parents reach driving age. Without efforts to prevent underage drinking, there could be an increase in the number of drunken driving deaths and injuries among these inexperienced drivers.

Additionally, research shows that the longer children's use of alcohol can be delayed, the less likely they are to become lifetime problem drinkers (and drunk drivers).

MADD also helped pass the federal 21 minimum drinking age and zero tolerance laws across the country. Formally embracing the prevention of underage drinking only strengthens MADD's commitment to youth. We will continue to partner with safety experts, educators, law enforcement, policymakers, parents and youth themselves to tackle underage drinking. Our nation's youth are tomorrow's leaders and we are investing in their future and ours."

2- How did MADD get started and how important is the problem it seeks to address?

"MADD was established by a group of women in California outraged after the death of a teenage girl killed by a repeat-offender drunk driver.

The issue is important: 18,000 people in American are killed every year in alcohol related crashes."

3- How successful is MADD?

"From its humble beginnings more than twenty years ago, MADD has evolved into one of the most widely supported and well-liked non-profit organizations in America. Since its founding, MADD has expanded from a group of angry activists marching on state capitals to a full-fledged, non-profit volunteer organization with an array of programs targeting a wide range of impaired driving, victim assistance, and underage drinking issues."

GRAPHICS AND LOGOS FOR SERVICE ORGANIZATIONS

Just as McLuhan's phrases "Global Village" and "The Medium is the Message" conveys concepts in word images, logos, brands and graphics visually communicate ideas and identity. Many students who wear T-shirts with graphics or literally "bare" tattooed graphics on their bodies are visually communicating their personal identity through symbols.

Mya Kramer, president of M Line Communications, created the graphics for Glide Church, the urban center for addressing the needs of the homeless and disadvantaged people in San Francisco. She suggests there are several ways to view the development of a graphic style, branding, and logo for organizations. Her ideas on design can be used by the speech communications student to improve how to understand the power of visual symbols as applied to conveying the identity of an organization in service to the community. She views branding of the non-profit organization the same way she does a corporation.

"You don't just see good design, you feel it. When design is paired with a strong concept, it reaches far beyond the eye, and sparks a more emotional and lasting response than either words or images alone. When we can touch the core spirit of the organization we can touch your audience.

The key to effective communication to any target is the ability to find and maintain the consistency of an authentic brand spirit, core and voice. That foundation, how it is built and applied to a brand platform, determines successful, long-term communication and brand development."

Kramer uses the phrase "Soul Branding" to illustrate the essence of identity building in communications. She states, 'Soul Branding' captures the authentic spirit and ethics of an organization. Take what is inside and making it visible to the audience.

• Vision and values should be visible.

• Unique is better. Even if there is a risk involved, find what is different in your brand personality and focus on it. The quirk will be appreciated.

• Brand is a living thing. Like a person, its core is constant, but its relationship with the audience can and should change and grow with the times. "

About Glide Church and Foundation

As a model of a community organization serving the homeless, disadvantaged, and discouraged, San Francisco-based Glide Church and Foundation is a thriving organization that serves these communities. It confirms the goodness and humanity in each person, and provides the resources and assistance to each individual to help themselves. The graphics developed by M Line Communications communicates these values. Even Glide's website communicates the values of inclusiveness and acceptance of all people. http://www.glide.org/

Quoted from their website, these are some of the programs Glide Church provides:

Meals

The largest of Glide's programs, the Free Meals Program serves three nutritious meals a day to the city's poor and homeless every day of the year. What began in 1969 as a Monday night potluck for 50 people now requires the talents of 27 staff members who come primarily from the ranks of the poor, homeless, formerly incarcerated and those with successful recovery from substances and addictions. The Free Meals Program utilizes one commercial-grade kitchen, two dining rooms, and tens of thousands of volunteers. It all adds up to over one million meals annually, all served in an environment of acceptance and respect.

Walk-in Center

A safe, welcoming space in the midst of the chaotic Tenderloin community. The Walk-In Center is Glide's resource center, a place where crises are calmed and questions answered. The highly-skilled Intake Specialists and counselors listen to each person's concerns, referring clients to Glide programs and community organizations that will give them the tools they need to help themselves. In their assessments, the staff treats the clients in a holistic manner. They understand that self-esteem, access to medical care, reliable housing options, childcare, and employment opportunities are integral pieces of a person's health and well-being.

Health

Building trust. Transforming lives. The Glide Health Clinic, Glide-Goodlett HIV/AIDS Project, and Glide Recovery programs all offer much more than treatment and advice. They give respect and support to people long accustomed to getting neither. Clients come to Glide's health programs with everything from a sprained ankle to a year-long recovery on the verge of relapse. Their stories are all unique, but the response is the same: acceptance, guidance, and unconditional love. A sense of belonging creates a feeling of hope. And a chance to be human again.

Housing

Hope. The CW House is alive with it. In the CW House's 52 modern apartments, lives are being rebuilt. It is a place where recovery liberates those enslaved by addiction. A place where joblessness is met by job training. Where children grow up in an atmosphere of education and community support. The hope is strong here. Because the homeless are finally coming home.

Family Services

Transportation, child care, medical insurance: Families without adequate support often find themselves bending or breaking from the pressures of daily living. The goal of Glide's Family Services programs is to support the entire family unit. Glide provides an extended family to grow with and a community to draw strength from. Everyone--from youth to seniors--is given the resources they need to realize their own power and potential.

Training & Employment Services

Today's job market is especially challenging for the thousands of poor and homeless individuals in the Bay Area . Glide's Training and Employment Services (TAES) program reaches out to the unemployed and under-trained with hands-on courses covering everything from computer programming to carpentry. Glide provides job skills training, interview skills, certification programs and assistance with job placement. Time and again, program graduates have proven that the only thing separating the homeless from the self-sufficient is the right set of tools.

In developing the images for T-shirts, water bottles, fans, and other everyday items, Kramer explains:

"Glide is an 'in your face' organization. They are about expressing things about the individual out in the open and working with people in a raw, human atmosphere. The philosophy of the church is to look for the best in people and help them to ascend. It is about humanity and spirit. The people who come to Glide are going to hopefulness and ascending in their behavior and self-esteem.

The idea of "Miracles in Action" is that miraculous things can happen if you take action. People, whom most of us would never give a chance to, will rise to the occasion though their encounter with Glide. It is not just about feeding and clothing people in need, but giving them a chance to start again."

Exercises

1. Create a five-person group presentation on Glide's program. Each person should speak about a different program within Glide, using the program information provided to show how Glide Church provides a whole system for working with the disadvantaged of San Francisco. Use the graphics developed by M Line to describe the spirit in Glide.

2. Each student should choose a local community organization (church, community center, or other non-profit). Develop a five minute speech using Mya Kramer's description of Glide as an "in your face" organization, their philosophy, and the "Miracles in Action" slogan and describe the way the organization you have chosen compares in its image with Glide's. Use a symbol or graphic from that organization if it has one.

Media communications can portray a powerful identity for a cause or organization. As we demonstrated with the "We Want Change Campaign" for advertising a cause to affect public policy and the Glide Church logo to communicate the identity of an organization, the same techniques in commercial media can be adopted for the service sector. Understanding the principles of media delivered communications as extensions of speech communication, the student can use the principles of USP, juxtaposition of known elements in a way, and "Soul Branding" to enhance their public speaking.

References

Mandelbaum, Michael (2002) Ideas That Conquered the World. Perseus Book Group, Cambridge, MA

McLuhan, Marshall, (1964) <u>Understanding Media: The Extensions of Man</u>, McGraw-Hill, New York.

Reeves, Rosscr, (1961) <u>Reality in Advertising</u> , Knopf, New York

CHAPTER 9

INTERCULTURAL COMMUNICATION IN SERVICE-LEARNING

Regardless of the course topic, service-learning projects often double as a lesson in intercultural communication. The very nature of service often requires you to work with people from a culture other than your own. That certainly proved the case for interpersonal communication students at Radford University who helped Bosnian refugees acclimate to the U.S., and for students from Colorado State University who did construction at the Pine Ridge Reservation in North Dakota. This also proved true for Winona State University service-learners taking a nonverbal communication course who tutored Hmong immigrants from Vietnam. But the same proved equally true for middle class, urban, black students at the University of Southern Mississippi who read to, and tutored underprivileged, rural, African American children, and for University of Missouri students who served meals to the homeless in a shelter just blocks from their dormitories. Encountering people with worldviews unlike yours and engaging in intercultural communication can happen just about anywhere.

Cultural variety enriches our lives while it simultaneously complicates the communication process. Culturally-based differences in gender role expectations, ethnicity, religious beliefs, country of origin, economic status, sexual orientation, nonverbal communication, perceptions about aging, and a host of other factors, influence our view of the world and our interaction with others. Yet regardless of the nature of the difference, you can, with knowledge, practice, empathy, and careful communication, successfully serve people from another culture while learning from them.

Although an entire book could be dedicated to intercultural communication factors of importance to service-learning, this chapter will focus on only a few, key subjects. Knowledge of these factors can improve your experience in service projects for any communication course. The information about intercultural communication presented here comes from Samovar & Porter's work (2000) Samovar, Porter, & Stefani's book (2000), an interview with Dr. Larry Samovar, discussions with other communication professors with experience in this area, and from student papers. Although a list of "dos and don'ts" would fail to cover the complexities of intercultural communication, the discussion below does introduce topics of relevance and general advice. They include:

- Ethnocentrism and Cultural Pride
- Beliefs, Attitudes and Values
- U.S. Cultural Patterns
- Nonverbal Communication and Culture
- Language, Verbal Communication and Culture
- Gender and Culture

ETHNOCENTRISM AND CULTURAL PRIDE

A scholar of intercultural communication for more than 40 years, Larry Samovar says the greatest obstacle to effectively working with people from other cultures is ethnocentrism. That word is so commonly used it is almost a cliché, he notes.

> But the truth is people commonly approach every culture other than their own believing, consciously or unconsciously, that 'Our (culture's) way is _the way_,' and that, 'Everyone else would be better off if only they did things our way too.' Ethnocentrism is really the notion that, where ever I go, whatever I do, I'm thinking, 'Why the hell do they do it that way? Why don't they do it the right way? _Our way_.'

Obviously, given the success of our species around the planet, there are many ways to live "the right way." When it comes to working with people from other cultures a "my-way-or-the-highway" mentality is not only ignorant; it is wrong, and antithetical to effective intercultural communication as well as service. Here is how one communication student at Hamlin University eloquently expressed this reality:

153

Intercultural communication is a two-way street. There is not a right and a wrong and it is not the responsibility of one or the other in an encounter to perfectly decipher the other's intentions. It is a learning exchange that requires an open mind and an ability to adapt. All of the reading in the world cannot prepare you for the "gut" reaction you have when your cultural "norms" are violated. We can prepare our minds for the inevitability of confusion and misinterpretation, but it is unreasonable, unnecessary, and egocentric to expect to be able to successfully decipher the culture that someone else has spent a lifetime living. Perhaps one of the most effective ways to deal with intercultural communication is to accept that misunderstandings will arise, but to honestly and insightfully evaluate our own internal cultural programming. We cannot begin to understand our differences if we cannot recognize the elements of ourselves that may be causing confusion. It is too easy to assign blame to "the other" if we are not aware of ourselves.

For most Americans the second great obstacle to effectively communicating and working with people of other cultures involves ignorance of others' pride. People commonly forget that "we" are not the only culture that takes great pride in our traditions, institutions, beliefs, norms, values, etc. For example, many Americans know that much of the rest of the world would like to emulate our dominant culture's material success. However, as Samovar puts it,

We mistakenly think that their desire for more material wealth represents an acceptance of all American culture. But even the poorest people in many other cultures do not want to adopt most of our main cultural themes and values. Many cultures have a greater interest than Americans do in spirituality, or maintaining strong extended-family ties, or in connecting with the natural world. Everyone wants a good place to live, enough to support their family's needs, and other basic benefits of material wealth. But that's about all many people of other cultures value and want to learn more about from the U.S.

Knowledge of others' cultural pride, those things that people of other cultures honor and value, increases an intercultural communicator's awareness, sensitivity and ability to empathize with others.

To achieve this level of awareness and respect one must withhold judgement when interacting with people from other cultures. Amaza Lieffort, a communication student who completed a service project, put it this way:

> *Although I hesitate to oversimplify such an immense topic, I still believe that respect is the key to harmonious intercultural interaction. When I say "respect", I am referring to an attitude or an internal mindset of open-mindedness and willingness to consider the point of view of the other.*

Respect is the attitude which suggests that one is aware that difference will exist but can be negotiated to the greater understanding of both parties. It suggests that difference in and of itself is not bad, but instead provides an opportunity for both sides to learn. It does not promise that everything will go smoothly every time, or that every difference will be easy to encounter, but does suggest that it is worthwhile to try. Most importantly, it does not judge or evaluate, but instead attempts to interpret objectively and subjectively to negotiate an acceptable middle ground which preserves the unique and stimulating differences of both sides and allows satisfying communication.

An effective intercultural communicator learns that there is more than one way to perceive and live in the world, and that judgments often must be made on the basis of the other's beliefs, attitudes and values rather than one's own.

BELIEFS, ATTITUDES, AND VALUES

Humans' sources of truth, their beliefs, shape almost every act of communication. Beliefs provide the core of our thoughts and actions. Often they may be based on a religious system, but beliefs can also be derived from a culture's history or economic, social, and political systems. Usually we take our beliefs for granted as "the truth;" they remain unquestioned, often unconsciously, because to question or reject a culture's beliefs can lead to punishment and ostracism. Beliefs also shape what cultures value and people's attitudes. Obviously, communication with someone from another culture may lead to misunderstanding and conflict, based on varied beliefs, attitudes, and values. Therefore, when working on a service project with people from a culture other than your own, it is important to be conscious of the dominant American cultural patterns that reflect common U.S. beliefs, attitudes, and values. The discussion below outlines these primary cultural patterns and provides examples of lessons students learned about these values while providing service (Samovar, Porter & Stefani, 2000a).

CULTURAL PATTERNS AND EXPECTATIONS

The most important, pervasive cultural pattern in the United States is individualism. Its manifestations in this country include self-reliance, personal initiative, independence, individual expression, and privacy rights. The culture teaches that the individual is the most important unit in any social setting. From cowboys to super models, from billionaire CEOs to superstar athletes, our role models reflect the dominant culture's identification with individualism. However, many other cultures value collectivism more highly, especially those in Africa, Asia, and Latin America. Collectivism stresses the importance of family, clans and organizations to look after people. Individuals exchange security for loyalty to the group. Collectivist cultures emphasize readiness to cooperate with members of the group, social expectations based on group roles, and group needs over individual desires. Rather than an "I" mentality, collectivist cultures stress a "we" outlook.

Equality, the belief that everyone has a right to success and that government should protect that right, is woven into the socio-political fiber of the culture. Americans emphasize the notion of social equality, both in the family and among friends and co-workers. Here, small power distance, informality and treating others the same no matter their age or social rank, erodes notions of hierarchy found in many other cultures. Of course, these statements about individualism and equality are generalizations about the culture. Americans do evaluate others based on income, race, social class, etc. However, we tend to do this less than is the case in cultures that value hierarchical structures and greater power distance, such as those in Germany, Japan and many Arab countries. People in such cultures believe it is naïve to ignore power and authority as facts of life, and that people are not equal; individual members of a culture have a particular place or role in the culture. These cultures centralize power, tend to respect authority figures and honor elders, place greater importance on rank, and by pass subordinates in decision-making.

Materialism pervades American culture. People expect to be well off – to have large wardrobes, televisions, cars, houses, computers, etc. We judge others based on their material success and take for granted our possessions. This stems in part from the consumer culture we have created via the mass production of goods and advertising. Additionally, we tend to view physical reality as the only reality – we consider the world of the five senses to be all there is. People from less materially wealthy cultures, including Brazil, Mexico and India, consider some of the poorest Americans to be materially rich, yet they also regard this culture as spiritually poor.

Science and technology have godlike status in the U.S. – we tend to believe technical experts, from doctors to physicists, can solve almost any problem. From roots in rationalistic philosophy, biblical injunctions to subdue the earth, and our pioneer ethic of conquering wilderness, this belief in technology leads to an assumption that reality and nature can, and should be governed by humans. The scientific method encourages people to try to predict and control much of life. Rationality, objectivity, and evidence are prized, while intuition and emotions are devalued because they lack scientific validity. Our belief in the inevitability of progress and change also stems largely from scientific and technological achievements. The "cult of progress" teaches that individuals, institutions, and nature, all can be improved upon with enough optimism, a focus on the future rather than the past, and "elbow grease." Belief in progress fosters acceptance of change, which, we assume, leads people in a new direction for the good. Consequently, this culture encourages risk-taking and staking out new opportunities.

More mature cultures, those that have evolved over thousands of years rather than hundreds, have seen civilizations rise and fall. Such cultures, notably Arab and Latin, tend to stress fatalism and uncertainty-avoidance, which is also common in Eastern cultures. Many of these cultures maintain that nature, not humans, determine one's fate, and that the most powerful forces of life fall outside of human control. God, fate, or magic rule in this worldview; such cultures teach that we must accept our destiny. The idea of shaping the future and of ignoring the past strikes members of these cultures as naïve and even arrogant. Still other cultures, for example Native American traditions, maintain that "the way" lies in cooperating with nature; it is neither a force to control nor one to merely accept, but a part of us to be affirmed as interconnected. Humans, such cultures teach, should seek to live in harmony with nature rather than subduing it.

Finally, Americans, perhaps more than any other culture, value work and competition. Even our leisure tends to be something we work at; often it is highly competitive. Work offers an avenue for recognition and a way to gain and control resources, which are important for individualistic cultures. Being the best (the most attractive, fastest, smartest, etc.) and being graded from kindergarten through college as well as thereafter, encourages Americans to compete. Other cultures, especially those that favor cooperation and group identity, such as in Mexico and Sweden, sometimes view typical American competitive behavior as ruthless, antagonistic and power-hungry.

VERBAL AND NONVERBAL COMMUNICATION ACROSS CULTURES

In addition to the dominant American cultural patterns, researchers have identified other patterns and verbal and nonverbal behavior that can lead to differences in perception and problems of communication. This next section presents common sources of tension for students who encounter these differences, verbal and nonverbal communication, when serving people from other cultures. The discussion includes explanations of some possible causes for the miscommunication. As a group, or class, you might discuss possible courses of action to improve the communication in these contexts.

- A person from another culture consistently shows up late for meetings. She or he arrives 15 to 45 minutes after the appointment. You find yourself increasingly frustrated and your indirect suggestions of displeasure do not appear to be having any effect.

Not all cultures live by the clock or teach that "time is money" and that "money makes the world go round." Cultures unconsciously teach people how to regard time. Informal rules for time, such as how late is "late," vary from culture to culture. For example, in Germany one shows respect for others by being a little early or right on time, while in Mexico showing up late for a business appointment communicates respect. The hurried pace of most Americans' lives strikes people of some other cultures as an obsession that borders on a social illness. Our culture also is future oriented. We plan for the future, think about what we're doing later today, or tomorrow, or a year from now, and can hardly wait to finish what we are doing so that we can move on to something else. We tend to be intolerant of delays – when we want something we want it now – but also innovative and open to change. On the other hand, past-oriented peoples, such as the Chinese, Arab, French, British and Native Americans, tend to resist change and look to the past for direction. Such cultures have long histories, so they tend to take a long-view of life and do not hurry decisions. They also venerate the elderly. Present-oriented cultures teach living in the moment.

Latin Americans and Filipinos, for example, tend to be more impulsive and spontaneous than others. Their lifestyle reflects a more fluid view of time and more relaxed pace. The Irish live by a present-oriented motto: "Life is a dance, not a race." Americans sometimes confuse this point of view with laziness and inefficiency. Our monochronic notion of time leads us to think of it as a tangible "thing" that must be managed and should not be wasted – you must not "lose time" or merely "kill time." Clocks, calendars, appointments, and schedules record the hours for work, school, and leisure. This gives us the sense that time is lineal and segmented. People in polychronic cultures (African, Arab, Asian, Latin) view time quite differently. Interaction with others takes priority over schedules. Because it is not considered tangible, few people consider time to be something that can be wasted. In the U.S., co-cultures relate to time more like polychronic cultures. Co-cultures, such as Hawaiian, Native American and African American, are groups within a society that shares many norms with the dominant culture but not power. Mainstream Americans may find people from such cultures and co-cultures confusing and frustrating because of their less structured, more spontaneous use of time.

- You work with someone from another culture that stands within two feet of you when talking. This makes you feel very uncomfortable but they appear to be comfortable and move closer when you back away.

A female college student working with a teenage male whose family immigrated from an Arab country noted this issue in a final paper for a service project. She wrote:

> *(Amin) reacted 'normally' to my signals of eye contact, and I responded 'normally' to his signals of proximity, but somewhere in the middle a misunderstanding arose. I was not trying to hit on him and he was not trying to make me uncomfortable, but that is what happened in spite of our awareness of our cultural differences.*

This illustrates difference in culturally-based nonverbal communication norms for personal space. The invisible boundaries around us we call "ours" communicate relationships to others. Individualistic cultures stress more space than communal cultures. Africans, Arabs and many Latin Americans typically communicate with others at much closer range than most North Americans consider comfortable and appropriate. Extended distance during interpersonal communication, as is found in some

Asian cultures, demonstrates esteem and deference. Extra distance also reflects privacy norms in Scotland and Scandinavia.

Cultures also modify the amount and direction of eye contact and gaze as well as appropriate touch. Most Americans value and expect direct eye contact, but it is not customary in all cultures. In some Asian cultures extensive direct eye contact can be interpreted as an insult or taboo. Caribbean, African and Latin American peoples communicate respect by avoiding eye contact. Arabs commonly look directly into the eyes of a communication partner for long periods to assess truthfulness and to show respect. However, between men and women this is considered a sign of sexual interest, as is the case in many cultures.

- An immigrant for whom English is a second language says something in a way that you consider socially inappropriate. She also expresses an idea with words you consider poorly chosen. You wonder if she understands the meaning of the word(s) and if she realizes the implications of how she has expressed them.

As Samovar and Porter note: "Language is the key to the heart of a culture." Learning how to use a new key takes many years of practice and frequent errors. As you know, words often have multiple denotative definitions and connotative meanings. (For example, say "dog," then ask a room of people what other word first comes to mind. You'll get a variety of answers that are based in varied experiences). The English language is vast and constantly changing, further complicating the issue. Additionally, the grammar rules of one language seldom make sense to people accustomed to another set.

Then there are the issues of translation, directness, emotive expression, enjoyment of language, and social relationships. Problems of translation and word-to-word equivalency can lead to countless misinterpretations. Dictionary translations do not convey the meaning of language when put to use, and certainly fail to communicate cultural nuances, slang, and idiomatic expressions. (Attempt explaining to someone from another culture statements such as, "Don't be a Monday morning quarterback," or "He's beating around the bush," or "McBigotry.") Translators – and service workers trying to help immigrants navigate our language – have to grapple with grammar and syntactical differences between languages as well as cultural differences in experience and attitude. Meanings for words come from shared experiences, so when we lack cultural equivalents we have no words to express ideas. For example, translating the phrase "She's got a poker face" into the Bulgarian language presents quite a challenge.

Obviously, translations frequently create misunderstanding for many reasons. If your service project will include use of translators to communicate with the people you serve, you should consider reading Samovar and Porter's discussion "Working with a Translator." You many find one of the rewards of serving people for whom English is a second language involve helping them understand that the meaning of their words does not always reflect their intent. One service-learning student noted that she had to explain to an immigrant that "I am a good lover" does not mean "I am friendly," and a male student had to inform a shy, reserved female from an Asian culture that, "You have an attractive voice" does not mean the same thing as, "Your voice sounds kind."

Directness suggests how quickly or bluntly people "get to the point." North Americans rarely speak with reserve. We tend to be unambiguous, honest, informal and explicit when we speak. Our use of language strikes people from some other cultures as uncaring for others, impolite, and uncivilized. Indirect language use seeks to preserve dignity, feelings and the "face" of others. Most cultures (Latin, African, Asian) use less directness than Americans do. Indirect politeness, such as avoiding open disagreement, is often regarded by North Americans as dishonest and detached, when it actually signals respect and an opportunity to save face. You can see how communication can become complicated by these different approaches.

Emotive expression and enjoyment of language distinguish cultural use of language even further. Americans tend to be more likely to express their emotions than members of some cultures, but less likely than members other cultures. For example, the British and Koreans seldom express emotions as openly or overtly as many North Americans. However, people from Latin and African cultures consider most North Americans to be emotionally reserved. Likewise, Europeans and Latin Americans get great pleasure from the art of conversation – verbal play and the ability to pontificate on any number of topics. "What many Americans may view as an uncomfortable confrontation best avoided, their European counterparts may see as an opportunity for passionate discussion, an intrinsic aspect of social life on the Continent," notes Alice Araujo, a professor who teaches intercultural communication at Mary Baldwin College. By American standards this form of "play" can sometimes look like combat. African and Arab cultures prize proverbs and have a deep love of language. To express an idea with eloquence, Arabic speakers may use 100 hundred words when an American might use 10. In this country, Russian immigrants have a reputation for making cutting comments that would not raise an eyebrow in their native culture. Obviously the emotional content of messages, and the feeling with which messages are communicated, varies from culture to culture.

Additionally, differences emerge from how cultures communicate social relationships via language use. Some tongues, such as Romanian and other romance languages, express status and relationship through separate verb conjunctions for the English word "you." Rigid social rules in Japanese society also apply to language use; separate vocabularies are used for addressing superiors, peers and inferiors, and a number of words take varied forms for different situations, sometimes depending on relationships between the communicators. Language use can even define gender roles in some cultures; pronunciation, grammar, vocabulary and context can vary based on gender.

- Your group works with refugees from a Baltic country. The women in your group are told to expect little attention from the refugee men, that they'll only be working with the women. In other words, your group will have to be segregated – men with men, women with women.

Just as what is means to be a man or woman in America today is very different from definitions of gender 25, 50 or 100 years ago, concepts of gender and appropriate role behavior for men and women varies from culture to culture (Wood, 2001). Cultures tend to value feminine or masculine traits more or less based on religious beliefs, politics, social history, and philosophy. Cultures that greatly value masculine behavior (such as achievement and acquisition of wealth, differentiated sex roles, and signs of manliness) teach men to be domineering, assertive and ambitious. Japan, Austria, Venezuela and Italy rank high on a scale of cultures that favor masculinity. In such countries men do most of the talking and decision making in social settings. Cultures that value femininity stress nurturing, protection for the environment, and sexual equality. Gender roles are more flexible, and interdependence and sympathy for the less fortunate is an ideal. Many Scandinavian cultures tend toward a feminine worldview.

One final note about gender. Few cultures stress gender equality as it is practiced in the U.S. Although sexism remains a reality here, American women have far more freedom and opportunity than women do in many other cultures. Your service work with people from other cultures may lead to concrete lessons in gender differences. For example, Professor Russell Lowery-Hart's communication students at West Texas A&M University run into problems based on gender differences almost every semester. He noted in an interview, "Students can research the group culture they will be working with, get the information about gender, etc. But until they actually experience socially constructed gender differences, that information isn't real to them. Service-learning makes it real." One student group in Lowery-Hart's class helped students from Philippines develop English language skills. The college students made judgements about the intelligence of women in the Filipino group because they were not participating, making eye contact, or discussing ideas in class. The men were doing all of the talking because to ask women to participate in a public discussion, even in class, would be asking them to violate cultural norms for their gender.

- When speaking with someone from another culture you find yourself doing most of the talking. You feel uncomfortable because of long silences and pauses before the other person speaks.

As a general rule, Americans abhor silence. We, like most Greeks, Italians, Arabs and Jews, fill silence with conversation when in the company of others. However, silence, in addition to serving as a cue in conversation, does "speak" in many cultures. Native Americans consider silence a sign of a great person; it also communicates respect to people of authority, age, or wisdom. Many Eastern traditions teach people to feel comfortable in the absences of noise and conversation. Indians, especially those who practice Hinduism, believe spiritual enrichment derives from silent meditation and introspection.

GENERAL ADVICE AND DISCUSSION

Differences in beliefs, cultural patterns, verbal and nonverbal communication, and gender, represent a fraction of the factors that complicate the communication process when working with people from other cultures and co-cultures. Take caution, but do not let this information intimidate you. Mistakes in communication across cultures are inevitable; mistakes also teach some of life's best lessons. So long as you show respect for others, chances are your service-learning project will allow you to learn much about people of another culture and communicate your good intentions. It also helps to follow several basic guidelines for listening and communicating mindfully. Julia Wood recommends emptying your mind of plans, concerns, and extraneous thoughts so that you are fully open to the other person. Concentrate on the person from the other culture by thinking to yourself, "I want to focus on this person, what she or he is thinking or feeling, not his or her costume, accent, color, etc." (Wood, 1999). To help prepare you for your intercultural service-learning assignment, your class or group might discuss the following "real life" scenarios faced by communication students doing service work:

1. What stereotypes do your have about the culture of the people you will be serving? What fears do you have about them, if any? What communication theories might explain stereotypes and/or fears about people from that culture?

2. How might you respond to the following intercultural communication scenarios that students have faced when doing service-learning projects?

3. While working with clients from another culture you are offered food that you've never eaten before. You do not find it very appealing, but people from the other culture are eating it and encouraging you to do the same.

4. A person you serve says something disparaging about your religion or culture. You find the comment highly offensive, but think that he does not understand the implications of his comments.

5. You arrive to your first meeting dressed as a typical American college student to find the people from another culture dressed in formal clothing. You do not feel comfortable. Before the next meeting you wonder how to dress.

6. Every time you shake hands with a person you serve you notice he or she has given you the "dead fish" grip – no pressure is returned. Your work includes helping her learn the cultural norms of North America for greetings and socially appropriate behavior.

7. While speaking to an immigrant from India, you notice the other person shaking his head "no" in response to much of what you have to say. But their verbal response suggests they agree with your comments.

8. You reach out to hug a student from Vietnam to congratulate her on improvements in English. She does not return the hug and appears very uncomfortable or embarrassed.

REFERENCES

Samovar, L., Porter, R. & Stefani, L. (2000). Communication between cultures (3rd ed.). San Francisco: Wadsworth.

Samovar, L., Porter, R. (2000). Intercultural communication (9th ed.). San Francisco: Wadsworth.

Wood, J. (1999). Interpersonal communication: Everyday encounters (2nd ed.). San Francisco: Wadsworth.

Wood, J. (2001). Gendered lives: Communication, gender, and culture (4th ed.). San Francisco: Wadsworth.

CHAPTER 10

SERVICE-LEARNING RESOURCES

SERVICE-LEARNING RESEARCH SOURCES AND PLACEMENT OPPORTUNITIES

The impressive national growth of service-learning has led to the development of many excellent Web sites that offer service-learning tutorials, journal articles, histories, course syllabi, essays, surveys and bibliographies. These sites form a network linking you to information covering virtually every facet of service-learning. If you wish to augment a service-learning project with scholarly research, instructor and student testimonials, or case studies, these sites should satisfy your need.

A number of sites also provide data-bases for placement opportunities. A student interested in service-learning usually first determines if a course instructor offers a list of placement opportunities and whether one is limited to those choices. In some cases instructors tailor a service-learning unit to the experience offered by a particular agency. In other cases a wider range of volunteer service is possible and an instructor may guide students to a campus career center or to an internship director with connections to community agencies. With the growth of service-learning, some campuses have offices providing placements specifically geared to support such curriculum. Offering the most flexible placement option, some courses permit students to contact any reputable community agency providing volunteer service that fulfills course objectives. In the Internet world this presents an endless range of choices. This section provides Web sites for a number of well-established national agencies that welcome volunteers. These Web sites provide numerous links to local branches and allied service agencies. But before contacting an agency offering an interesting sounding experience, use the following questions to determine if the opportunity provides a good fit for your course:

1. Can I review literature that may help me decide which agency best meets my needs?
2. Can I clearly explain my service-learning goals to the agency's volunteer coordinator?
3. Do I have a syllabus of course objectives with me when I contact the agency or meet with its representative?
4. Will the agency provide adequate supervision and complete required contract and evaluation forms?

If you obtain positive responses to these questions, your self-guided search of agencies will likely lead to a rewarding experience.

SERVICE-LEARNING RESOURCE SITES

America's Promise
www.americaspromise.org/
The alliance for Youth formerly led by General Colin Powell, is dedicated to mobilizing individuals, groups and organizations from every part of American life, to build and strengthen the character and competence of our youth. The Alliance provides information and publishes progress reports by its partners.

American Association of Community Colleges (AACC) Service Learning
www.aacc.nche.edu/servicelearning/
The site provides links to general information on service learning, upcoming workshops, links to organizations related to service learning and higher education, and a link to AACC's Service Learning Project.

American Association for Higher Education (AAHE) Service Learning Project
www.aahe.org and www.aahe.org/service/srv-lrn.htm

AAHE is the individual membership organization that promotes the changes higher education must make to ensure its effectiveness in a complex, interconnected world. The association equips individuals and institutions committed to such changes with the knowledge they need to bring those changes about. AAHE is actively engaged in promoting service learning through conferences, trainings, and the Service Learning Monograph Series.

American Educational Research Association
www.aeranet/
The American Educational Research Association is concerned with improving the educational process by encouraging scholarly inquiry related to education and by promoting the dissemination and practical application of research results.

Association for Experiential Education
www.aee.org/
The Association for Experiential Education (AEE) is a non-profit, international professional organization that is committed to the development, practice and evaluation of experiential education in all settings.

Association for Supervision and Curriculum Development, The
www.ascd.org
ASCD is an international, nonprofit, nonpartisan education association committed to the mission of forging covenants in teaching and learning for the success of all learners. Founded in 1943, ASCD provides professional development in curriculum and supervision; initiates and supports activities to provide educational equity for all students; and serves as a world-class leader in education information services.

Campus Compact
www.compact.org
Campus Compact is a national alliance of colleges and universities interested in promoting service and leadership at their institutions. Its Web page includes syllabi of courses with service dimensions, full text of and order forms to its publications, and job postings related to service and higher education.

Campus Compact National Center for Community College
www.mc.maricopa.edu/academic/compact/
The organization serves as a national advocate for community colleges in service learning and assists organizations with the promotion and implementation of community service. The web site provides staff information, announcements of award winners, links to related organizations

and schools, full text and ordering information of its publications, and information on its conferences and projects.

Close Up Foundation
www.closeup.org
Close Up's mission is built on the belief that textbooks and lectures alone are not enough to help students understand the democratic process and make it work. Students need a "close up" experience in government. Close Up's national, state and local experiential government studies programs strengthen participants' knowledge of how the political process works, increase their awareness of major national and international issues, and motivate them to become actively involved in the world around them.

Community Activities Resources Environment Services (CARES)
http://library.thinkquest.org/50017
A well organized website that provides information about service-learning. The site includes a description of service-learning; how to organize and construct service-learning projects; examples of model lesson plans and service-learning projects; links to other service-learning sites and a bibliography.

Community-Campus Partnerships for Health (CCPH)
http://futurehealth.ucsf.edu/ccph.html
CCPH is nonprofit organization founded in 1996 to foster health-promoting partnerships between communities and educational institutions. CCPH identifies students, institutional leaders and community leaders as equal constituencies, and we serve as a welcoming bridge between the many government and foundation-sponsored initiatives in community-oriented health professions education.

Compact for Learning and Citizenship
www.az.com/~pickeral/talkingpoints.html
The Compact for Learning and Citizenship, developed in 1997, is an organization of state chiefs and superintendents committed to creating a public voice, developing policy, and communicating the integral role service and service-learning play in K-12 student academic achievement and civic development. They believe that K-12 teachers should be provided the formal opportunity to understand the principles and good practices of service-learning, through opportunities such as pre-service teaching training and/or in-service professional development.

Corporation for National and Community Service
www.cns.gov
The Corporation for National and Community Service (CNS) is a federal agency that works with state governments and community organizations to provide opportunities for Americans of all ages to serve through AmeriCorps, Learn and Serve, and National Senior Service Corps programs.

Council of Independent Colleges – Service-Learning Related Publications
www.cic.edu/newspubs/catalog/
Explore this web page which contains various service-learning publications, some of which have the full text available to print out.

Generations United
www.gu.org
Generations United provides information about intergenerational initiatives around the country (both Learn and Serve and other types of programs). Generations United, as a clearinghouse itself, coordinates information for over 130 intergenerational efforts.

International Partnership for Service-Learning
www.studyabroad.com/psl/
The International Partnership for Service-Learning is an incorporated not-for-profit organization serving colleges, universities, service agencies and related organizations around the world by fostering programs that link community service and academic study. IPS-L also organizes conferences on the development of service-learning, promotes the principles and practice of service-learning by encouraging partnership relationships, and publishes materials related to service-learning. Their web site contains information about their programs.

Learn and Serve America
www.learnandserve.org/
Learn and Serve America is one of the "streams of service" administered by the Corporation for National Service. Learn and Serve America offers grants for service-learning programs in institutions of higher education, K-12 schools, and community based organizations.

Learning In Deed
www.learningindeed.org

This initiative, launched in 1998 by the W.K. Kellogg Foundation, aims to make service-learning part of every K-12 student's experience.

Michigan Journal of Community Service Learning, The
www.umich.edu/~mjcsl/
The Michigan Journal of Community Service Learning (MJCSL) is a peer-reviewed journal consisting of articles written by faculty and service-learning educators on research, theory, pedagogy, and issues pertinent to the service-learning community.

National Communication Association
www.natcom.org
The NCA has a long history of commitment to service-learning in communication studies. This site provides service-learning resources developed by NCA members as part of a three-year grant from the American Association for Higher Education and Campus Compact. Excellent resources for implementing service-learning across the speech communication discipline.

National Dropout Prevent Center
www.dropoutprevention.org
National Dropout Prevention Center at Clemson University serves as the Regional Information Center for the southern portion of the country, providing information about programs in eleven southern states. They also provide access to the National Dropout Prevention Network, a large organization that provides information on dropout prevention, and also the use of service-learning programs to help young people achieve success in school.

National Service-Learning Exchange, The
www.lsaexchange.org/
The Learn and Serve America Exchange, led by the National Youth Leadership Council supports service-learning programs in schools, colleges and universities, and community organizations across the country through peer-based training and technical assistance. If you need assistance implementing service-learning programs, have questions, or simply want to speak with someone who has "been there," you can utilize the Exchange as a resource by calling toll-free 1-877-572-3924.

National Service-Learning Clearinghouse

www.servicelearning.org/
A comprehensive information system that focuses on all dimensions of service-learning, covering kindergarten through higher education school-based as well as community based initiatives. The Center of the Clearinghouse is located at the University of Minnesota, Department of Work, Community and Family Education, with collaboration from a consortium of twelve other institutions and organizations.

National Service-Learning Partnership
www.servicelearningpartnership.org
The Partnership's purpose is unique: it is to orchestrate a comprehensive and broad-based approach to making service-learning a standard part of students' education across the United States. As a network of grassroots and national service-learning supporters, the Partnership brings together organizational and individual members, including thousands of practitioners, administrators, community activists, policymakers, researchers, parents, young people and leaders in business and other sectors.

National Service Resource Center
www.etr.org/nsrc
The National Service Resource Center (NSRC) is a training and technical assistance provider to programs funded by the Corporation for National Service. This web site contains a resource library, a master calendar, resource guides, online documents, sample forms collection, newsletters, and America Reads resources.

National Society for Experiential Education
www.nsee.org
The National Society for Experiential Education (NSEE) is a membership association and national resource center that promotes experienced-based approaches to teaching and learning. For over 25 years, NSEE has developed best practices for effectively integrating experience into educational programs. NSEE works with educators, businesses, and community leaders in the shared belief that students' full learning potential can most effectively be tapped through experience-based education programs.

Points of Light Foundation
www.pointsoflight.org
The Points of Light Foundation meets the practical learning needs of individuals and organizations that seek to engage volunteers in community

service efforts. The Foundation's mission is to engage more people more effectively in volunteer community service to help solve serious social problems.

SERVENet
www.servenet.org
A program of Youth Service America, this is a free service bringing together volunteers and community organizations. Post and search for volunteer opportunities nationwide.

Service Leader
www.serviceleader.org
Extensive, comprehensive resources to help agencies involve volunteers via the Internet. Includes materials to help service leaders use the Internet to work with and better serve both online and onsite volunteers. Volunteer management and community engagement resources. Links to several major volunteer related online resources, a resource guide for schools, and a Susan Ellis section on the volunteer experience.

Service Learning: Education Beyond the Classroom
www.epa.gov/epaoswer/general/educate/svclearn.htm
This booklet, provided by the U.S. Environmental Protection Agency, describes how students across the country are gaining hands-on awareness of waste reduction, recycling and composting through solid waste service-learning projects.

Volunteer Match
www.volunteermatch.org/
VolunteerMatch is the nonprofit, online service that helps interested volunteers get involved with community service organizations throughout the United States. Volunteers enter their ZIP code on the VolunteerMatch web site to quickly find local volunteer opportunities matching individual interests and schedules. This simple, effective service has already generated hundreds of thousands of volunteer referrals nationwide.

Youth Service America
www.ysa.org/
A resource center and alliance of 200+ organizations committed to increasing the quantity and quality of opportunities for young Americans to serve locally, nationally and globally.

GUIDELINES FOR CONTACTING THE SERVICE AGENCY

Typically, you initiate communication with a prospective or selected service agency. Whether soliciting a placement or contacting the agency that has selected you, note certain communication protocols.

Recognize that many community service agencies are understaffed and extremely busy. Don't be dismayed if your call is not immediately returned. Exercise persistence and call back soon.

Professionals often prepare for phone communication. Before you call, outline the important details of your message. If you reach the correct individual or leave a message, have a planned introduction ready. Note the following example.

> *Hello, my name is. I am presently enrolled in a group communication course at _____ University. Professor _____ gave me your name and number. I'm very interested in volunteering as a recreation leader for your agency. I want to apply the group communication principles I am learning in class to the volunteer position. When can I meet with you to discuss this further?*

If you leave a message, again, remember that the agency may be slow in returning your call. Your selection of a particular organization reflects your interest in its activities. Practice persistence by leaving a follow-up message stating your continuing interest, your phone number, and times of availability.

Chapter 1 addressed the need to cultivate a professional attitude. Thoughtfully planning contact with a community agency is part of a professional approach.

STUDENT JOURNAL GUIDELINES

Chapter 1 described the central role of journal writing to the reflection component of service-learning. Various chapters have presented extracts from student journals illustrating how reflective writing provides a means for recording duties, skill development, personal feelings, and analyzing experiences through the prism of communication theory.

A well-written journal provides rich illustration. Transport the reader to the service scene, vividly describing specific experiences in detail. Avoid unsupported generalizations and simplistic application of theory. For example, a student working on a brochure for an ethnic art museum wrote,

> *"The museum's membership data provided information on the occupation, education level, and special interests of current members. This helped me generate an approach for a brochure designed to interest new members."*

This journal entry missed the opportunity to address audience analysis in greater depth, the cornerstone of persuasive communication. The entry also omitted a descriptive profile of current members revealed by the museum's data and specific communication strategies that might appeal to potential members. Remember to add supportive detail to general statements.

Your instructor may indicate the expected frequency of journal contributions. The guidelines below provide a model encouraging in-depth journal entries, including descriptions of service responsibilities, skills learned, personal reflections, and observations of applied communication concepts and theories.

SERVICE-LEARNING JOURNAL GUIDELINES

Reflective writing is an important means for connecting your volunteer experience to course content. Your journal involves more than simply logging events. You should describe your duties, interactions, impressions, and supply communication analyses that apply principles presented in class readings, lectures, and discussions. Your instructor may include specifically tailored questions to help you integrate your experiences with course concepts. Journals will be reviewed periodically by your instructor. Your reflections will help you add to class and group discussions.

Your journal should address how your volunteer experience related to, or contrasted with, course concepts and affected your view of the material presented in class. Additionally, describe ways in which course concepts/skills are relevant to performing community activities.

Consider the following model to help organize your entries:

Introduction

Your introduction should briefly preview what you will cover in the entry. You should also include a general background that establishes a context for the entry.

Description

Describe a specific field experience. Describe the experience with sufficient detail so the reader understands with whom you interacted, the effects of the interaction, and your feelings about the experience or task. Do not yet analyze your experience-simply describe it.

Interpretation/Analysis

After completing the above, make interpretations of the experience. Analyze the experience as it relates to the theories, principles, or concepts you have studied in this course.

Response

If appropriate, conclude your entry by briefly addressing the following:

Based on my volunteer experience to date, and in an effort to grow as a communicator, I will attempt to:

Discontinue:

Begin to Practice:

Continue to Practice:

The following reflection ideas may help you write substantive entries.

1. What do your service duties entail?
2. Are your service duties meeting your expectations? Explain.
3. Describe the most satisfying parts of your experience.
4. Describe the most difficult aspects of your experience.
5. How is your service relevant to class readings, lectures and discussions?
6. What skills (human/technical) are you learning?

7. Does your service have an impact?
8. How has your perception of the community been affected by your experience?
9. How will this experience be of value to your future?
10. How can you make others more aware of community needs that you recognize?
11. What advice would you provide a future student performing similar service?

GUIDELINES FOR STUDENT EVALUATION OF SERVICE EXPERIENCE

Upon completing your service assignment, your evaluation of your placement involves more than a closure of the service experience. As the person in the field, your evaluation of the quality and benefits of your placement provides vital feedback for your instructor. Your evaluation of acquired skills, quality of supervision and training, logistical demands, etc., may influence your instructor's communication with the agency.

If your instructor sees a problematic pattern emerge form student evaluations, corrective measures can be taken. Conversely, a community agency consistently praised by students for providing a rewarding experience should receive recognition from your instructor and institution. This is part of maintaining a productive relationship between the campus and the community. Take this evaluation seriously. It is a vital component of maintaining the high quality of a service-learning program.

Student Evaluation of Service-Learning Experience

Student's Name_____

Volunteer Agency_____

Directions

Answer the following questions fully, adding as much detail as possible. Your comments will not influence your grade. Attach an additional page if you require extra space.

1. What was the most beneficial aspect of the service-learning component of this course?

2. Can you identify any important areas the instructor failed to cover that would have strengthened the connection between community service and classroom learning?

3. What two or more things would you do differently in the reflection component of the course?

4. Did you receive adequate supervision at your community placement?

5. Was the agency clear and fair in its representation of your responsibilities?

6.   How would you describe the communication climate at the agency?

7.   Did you receive periodic feedback from your supervisor?

8.   Was the agency fair in its evaluation of your performance?

9.   What useful skills or experiences did you acquire that will complement your academic studies or enhance your career prospects?

10.   What changes could the agency make to improve its coordination of volunteers?

11.   Would you recommend this agency to a future student?

COMMUNITY PLACEMENT FIELD AGREEMENT

For the benefit of all participating parties, a contract, the Community Placement Field Agreement, is developed and signed by all participating parties, the student, the agency supervisor, and the course instructor. This contract formalizes the volunteer process and clarifies the responsibilities of all participants.

Community Placement Field Agreement

Student Name _____

Course _____ Semester/Year _____

Student's Phone Number _____

Student's E-mail Address_____

Agency's Name _____

Agency's Phone Number _____Fax _____

Name of Agency Supervisor _____

I, _____ agree to:
Student's Name

1) _____ hours of community service in this agency beginning no later

   than _____and continuing through _____

2) My activities and work expectations for this placement will be
   _____
   _____
   _____

3) The learning objectives connected to this placement are:
   (example: increase understanding of diverse cultures by tutoring youth)
   _____
   _____

4) I will comply with the agency rules set forth by the supervisor. I will serve in a professional manner with respect for others. I will be on time, call the placement if I cannot attend due to illness, and will carry out assigned and agreed upon tasks or services. I will abide by all policies of the placement, especially with regard to confidentiality.

5) I will perform the work assigned to me, which should be worthwhile and challenging, provide input for improvement on my assignments, and follow organizational policies and procedures.

6) If I encounter any difficulties or concerns regarding this assignment I will contact _____my course professor.

On behalf of _____, I agree:
                                  Agency's Name

A. To provide orientation and necessary training to the student, thereby stating clearly the goals of the program/agency and the needs of the population served.

B. To provide clear goals of the placement opportunity to the student.

C. To contact, _____ course professor, with questions, concerns, and/or feedback about this project or the student.

Together, we agree that the above student will serve in the above named placement, beginning _____ and ending _____, on the following day(s) during the week/weekend _____ at the specific time(s) _____.

Student Signature _____ Date _____

Placement Supervisor Signature _____ Date _____

Faculty Signature _____ Date _____

Student: Please Fill-Out and Return To Faculty Advisor

SUPERVISOR EVALUATION FORM

At the conclusion of the volunteer experience, the field supervisor evaluates the student's performance at the participating agency. In addition to this written evaluation the supervisor ideally provides regular oral feedback to the student volunteer.

Supervisor Evaluation Form

Name of Agency _____

Field Supervisor Name _____

Student's Name: _____

Total Hours Completed: _____

1. **INSTRUCTIONS:** Please rate the student in the following areas: (**1**=Unsatisfactory, **2**= Barely Acceptable, **3**=Satisfactory, **4**=Good, **5**=Excellent, **n/a**=not applicable, or don't know).

    A. Student fulfilled her/his learning goals and objectives
        1 2 3 4 5 n/a

    B. Student was mature/professional relations with staff
        1 2 3 4 5 n/a

    C. Student was punctual
        1 2 3 4 5 n/a

    D. Student was sensitive to confidentiality issues
        1 2 3 4 5 n/a

    E. Student was aware of agency mission
        1 2 3 4 5 n/a

    F. Student had motivation and interest in assigned responsibilities
        1 2 3 4 5 n/a

G. Student attended to tasks assigned to him or her
    1 2 3 4 5 n/a

H. Student, once trained, was able to function independently
    1 2 3 4 5 n/a

I. Student handled self well in problem situations
    1 2 3 4 5 n/a

J. Student was dependable
    1 2 3 4 5 n/a

K. Overall performance and effectiveness of this student
    1 2 3 4 5 n/a

2. How prepared was the student for her/his service at your agency (e.g., skills, ability to take on new challenges, ability to work in a group setting, etc.)? How could the student have prepared to volunteer at your agency? (Feel free to continue on back.)

3. Once trained, comment specifically on areas of the student's performance that need improvement and what he/she can do differently. (Feel free to continue on back.)

Completed by _____ Title _____
                    Name

Signature _____ Date _____

Thank you for your time in completing this evaluation and your participation in the project. I hope that we may work together in the very near future.

AUTHOR BIOGRAPHIES

Rick Isaacson is Internship Director and Service-Learning Coordinator for the Department of Speech and Communication Studies at San Francisco State University. He teaches courses including Persuasion, Speech for the Classroom Teacher, Rhetoric of the Media, and Group Discussion. His students have pursued service-learning activities in a variety of community agencies, including homeless shelters, convalescent homes, mediation centers, public health agencies and mentoring and literacy programs. He finds that volunteering often inspires the most compelling student speeches, essays, and journals, as community service dispels many preconceptions students bring to their service experience. You can contact him at isaacson@sfsu.edu.

Jeff Saperstein is a consultant, marketing instructor, and author working in the public, nonprofit and private sectors. He is a veteran professional with thirty years experience in marketing and communications. Jeff is an adjunct instructor in marketing and has taught business professionals in Latin America, France, Israel, Japan, the San Francisco State Graduate School of Business, Stanford University Professional Development, and UC Berkeley Extension. More about his work at www.creatingregionalwealth.com.

He is co-author of:

Creating Regional Wealth in the Innovation Economy: Models, Perspectives and Best Practices, Prentice Hall, 2002.

How to be a More Effective Account Manager: Advertising and Public Relations, Kentwood Publications, 1989.

Practical Approaches to Impromptu Speaking: Social and Business Applications, Kendall Hunt, 1988 (co-authored with Rick Isaacson)

In their work together, Rick brings thirty years of university experience teaching speech communication, and Jeff provides the workplace experience of thirty years in the corporate, nonprofit and public sectors.

Both are Mill Valley, California residents and avid hikers, frequently seen on Marin County trails in rapturous conversation.